FROM BAGHDAD TO BOSTON AND BEYOND

FROM BAGHDAD TO BOSTON AND BEYOND

MEMOIR OF AN IRAQI JEW

JACOB B. SHAMMASH

Edited by Amy S. Dane

FROM BAGHDAD TO BOSTON AND BEYOND
MEMOIR OF AN IRAQI JEW

iUniverse books may be ordered through booksellers or by contacting:

iUniverse
1663 Liberty Drive
Bloomington, IN 47403
www.iuniverse.com
1-800-Authors (1-800-288-4677)

ISBN: 978-1-5320-4640-7 (sc)
ISBN: 978-1-5320-4641-4 (e)

Library of Congress Control Number: 2018903734

Print information available on the last page.

iUniverse rev. date: 04/25/2018

Dedication

My book is dedicated to my wife, 5 children,
their spouses and my 10 grandchildren:

Amy and Steven Dane and their children, Caroline and Matthew
Deborah Shammash and Scott Soloway and
their children, Benjamin and Sydney
Ellen Shammash and Douglas Hotvedt and their
3 daughters, Sarah, Amanda and Rachel
Jonathan Shammash and Rebecca Baxt and their
children, Naomi, Gabrielle and Zachary
Elizabeth Shammash and David Reed

A special thanks goes to my wife Estelle. She has been
my love and my companion for over 60 years. Without her
encouragement, I wouldn't have completed my story for
publication. It is with that same persistence that she helped
our children succeed through school, activities, interests and
their professional lives. They say that "behind every man is
a good woman." That has certainly been the case in my life.
Every Friday night at the Sabbath table I sing her my praises.

Contents

Daily Prayers

A Historical Perspective

My father, Jacob B. Shammash, was born in Baghdad in 1927 to a wealthy businessman and land owner. Jake, as he is called, was the third of 9 children. Large families were typical there and then, whether Jewish or Muslim.

The picture of him on the opposite page shows him performing his daily prayers. He grew up in a family steeped in Jewish faith and tradition, a faith he has embraced his entire life. Today he is one of the most religious members of his family, practicing the rituals his grandfather taught him many years ago. The value system he grew up with shaped both his career path and his moral character.

The Jewish community in Baghdad extended back to the destruction of the first temple in Jerusalem in 586 BCE (Before the Common Era) and the Babylon captivity over 2,600 years ago. By the time my dad was 12, one-third of the population of Baghdad was Jewish. Only a handful of Jews, if any, remain there today.

Although Abraham, the Patriarch, had lived with his clan in the Ur of Chaldees in Sumer, he had been called away by God to establish the new religion of one God in the land we now call Israel. There they lived until the Jews of the Kingdom of

Judah were exiled to Babylon in 3 successive waves during the 6th century BCE, starting with the destruction of the temple in Jerusalem in 586 BCE by the Babylonian King Nebuchadnezzar.

The Jews were faced with a dilemma: how were they to survive and become successful in their new home and yet maintain their unique culture and religion? Psalm 137 begins with a lament that expresses this perplexing question:

> *By the rivers of Babylon*
> *There we sat down, yea, we wept*
> *When we remembered Zion. ...*
> *And those who plundered us required of us mirth,*
> *Saying, "Sing us one of the songs of Zion!"*
> *How shall we sing the Lord's song*
> *In a foreign land?*

In his book, *The Last Jews in Baghdad: Remembering a Lost Homeland*, author Nissim Rejwan quotes the advice given in a letter by the prophet Jeremiah (29:5-7) to these perplexed Jews[1]:

> *Build houses and live in them; plant gardens and eat their*
> *produce. Take wives and have sons and daughters...multiply*
> *there and do not decrease. But seek the welfare of the city*
> *where I have sent you into exile and pray to the Lord on*
> *its behalf, for in its welfare you will find your welfare.*

This pragmatic strategy allowed them to prosper, but to keep their religion vital, they had to write down and memorize their

---

[1] Rejwan, Nissim. "The Last Jews of Baghdad: Remembering a Lost Homeland". University of Texas Press, 2004, p. 209.

stories and traditions—a necessity which led to the eventual creation of the Talmud. They had witnessed the destruction of the temple. Thus their religion could not be centered on a building and the rituals it contained. It had to become more inwardly focused on moral precepts, moral actions, defining customs, and close relationships which could withstand the vagaries of outer political turmoil.

In 539 BCE when King Cyrus of Persia conquered Babylonia, he allowed the exiled Jews to return to Jerusalem and rebuild their temple. Even though this change of fortune was welcomed, Nissim Rejwan points out that the majority of the exiles did not *want* to return since they were already prosperous and established in business and farming.[2] Those who stayed contributed gold and silver for the rebuilding of Jerusalem and the temple.

Eventually, as the Talmud was being compiled there were two versions—the Babylonian Talmud and the Jerusalem Talmud, indicating 2 loci of authority and 2 ways of keeping Jewish identity intact. The Babylonian community became the model for a successful diaspora community living as a minority in a land swept by storms of successive rulers. Refugees from the rebellion against Rome in 73CE (Common Era) and later the Spanish expulsion of 1492 added to the community. During the Ottoman period, due to the enforced tolerance of diverse groups, the Jews in Baghdad prospered and grew in numbers. When the British Mandate began in 1920, their business interests, particularly in trade, meshed with the British colonial policies.

When Iraq was established as an independent country in

---

[2] Ibid. p. 210.

1932, the guarantees of equality before the law, which had been guaranteed by the liberal 1925 constitution, continued to be enforced. Minority communities were allowed to establish their own schools and practice their own customs unimpeded. Both Jewish and Arab communities prospered during this period which the Shamash family remembers well. During this liberal period the Baghdad community managed to balance the tension between assimilation and the preservation of a Jewish identity.

After this long history of 28 centuries, it was ironic and shocking that this community should be accused of disloyalty to Iraq and subjected in 1941 to a Nazi-inspired pogrom called the Farhud. When Israel was founded in 1948, the policies of expulsion from which the Shamash family suffered, were a cruel reversal of the long ago Babylonia captivity lamented by the prophets and psalmists.

The new model of the diaspora was lived out by the Shamash family's resettling in America. My father tells his story, a story I only heard just several years ago. Now I understand why. So much of it was and still is very painful. One thing is clear; all of them helped each other to the extent possible. My father was the first to arrive in the United States. Even though he was a recent immigrant and just starting college, he began doing all he could to help his family back home. As his brothers and sisters left one by one to attend college, they located near each other and gave one another full support. All of them became successful and in good part, can thank each other for that.

Amy S. Dane (with assistance from Ellen Peck)

MODERN IRAQ

1534-1918 Ottoman rule of the Arab section of Iraq. The Kurds and Persian sections of Iraq were separate. During the 19ᵗʰ century British influence increased. The Jewish community was allowed to establish schools and generally supported the Ottoman rule.

1914-1918 During World War I a conflict developed between supporters of Germany and patrons of Britain.

1918 Three sections—Mosul, Baghdad, and Al-Basrah—were put together as one country during the peace negotiations. The medieval name "Iraq" was chosen—the Arab name for the general region.

1920 At the San Remo conference Britain received the League of Nations' British Mandate of Palestine.

1921 Faisal was installed as a constitutional monarch under the British Mandate. Liberal reforms were instituted allowing the Jewish community to prosper.

1924-25 Iraq constructed its first constitution and its first parliament was elected.

1932 Full independence was gained with the end of the British Mandate.

1933-39 Rule of King Ghazi who was killed in an auto accident. His young son Faisal II was crowned king under a regent.

1940-41 During World War II conflicts developed again over loyalty to Germany or Britain. Rashid Ali, the military leader favoring Germany and Arab nationalism, stirred anti-Jewish feelings leading to a pogrom.

1941 On June 1st and 2nd a pogrom called the Farhud (violent dispossession) was carried out against the Jewish community in Baghdad. Hundreds of people were killed, thousands injured and property damages were estimated at $3 million (the equivalent of $50 million in 2018).

1947 On November 29th The United Nations approved the creation of a Jewish State and an Arab State in the British Mandate of Palestine.

1948 On May 14th the State of Israel declares itself an independent Jewish state hours before the British Mandate is due to expire.

The following actions took place in Iraq that year:

- July: The government passed a law making all Zionist activity punishable by execution, with a minimum sentence of 7 years imprisonment.
- August 28th: Jews were forbidden to engage in banking or foreign currency transactions

- September: Jews were dismissed from the railways, the post office, the telegraph department and the Finance Ministry on the grounds that they were suspected of "sabotage and treason."
- October 8th: Issuance of export and import licenses to Jewish merchants was forbidden.
- October 19th: The discharge of all Jewish officials and workers from all governmental departments was ordered.
- October: The Egyptian paper, El-Ahram, estimated that as a result of arrests, trials and sequestration of property, the Iraqi treasury collected some 20 million dinars ($80 million)

1950

- March: The government of Iraq passed the Denaturalization Act allowing Jews to emigrate if they renounced their Iraqi citizenship. Iraqi Prime Minister Tawfiq al-Suwaidi expected that 7,000–10,000 Jews out of the Iraqi Jewish population of 125,000 would leave.
- March: an airlift mounted by Israel called Operations Ezra and Nehemiah (1950-52) took 75% of the Jewish community (between 120,000 and 130,000 people) to Israel. After 1952 Jews were forbidden to leave the country.
- April: A series of synagogue bombings began.

1952 Although the Denaturalization Act of 1950 was extended, emigration was banned.

1963 Under the Ba'ath Party, more restrictions were placed on remaining Iraqi Jews. Sale of property was banned. Jews had to carry yellow identity cards.

1967 After the Six-Day War, Jewish property was expropriated, bank accounts were frozen, Jews were dismissed from public posts, their businesses were closed and other restrictions were imposed.

1969 Public hanging of 14 men, including 9 Jews, who were falsely accused of spying for Israel.

1970 Early in the 70's, bowing to international pressure, the Iraqi government allowed most of the remaining Jews to emigrate.

1979 Saddam Hussein gained control under the Ba'ath Party. By then only 400 Jews were left in Baghdad.

2003 In the aftermath of the Iraq War the Jewish Agency estimated that there were only 34 Jews left in Baghdad.

Present estimates of the Jewish Population in Baghdad:

2007: 7
2008: 5
2013: 5

2014 The Babylonian Heritage Center in Tel Aviv was opened.

By their estimates, the number of Jews of Baghdad heritage living in Israel (as reported by the New York Times in 2016): 227,900
More information can be found on the following websites:
https://en.wikipedia.org/wiki/History_of_the_Jews_in_Iraq

https://en.wikipedia.org/wiki/Timeline_of_Jewish_history

http://www.bjhcenglish.com/about-us

https://www.haaretz.com/us-news/u-s-to-return-jewish-artifacts-to-iraq-despite-protests-1.5449538

Preface

I sit in the cage-like protrusion that guards a second story window of our home as I watch the happenings below. We live in the inner city of Baghdad on a narrow street that leads into the Shorjah, the largest market place in Baghdad. It is the early 1930s. I am 5 years old, more or less. My mother often left one of her small children to entertain himself as I am doing today, watching the hustle and bustle of people funneling into the congestion of the Shorjah to haggle for their wares.

It is early morning on a warm spring day. Directly under my window I spot a man guiding his a large camel, laden with goods. A gentle push by the master to the camel's front leg at the knee signals the animal to sit. The beast eases itself to the ground by first bending its front legs, followed by the rear ones. The animal begins regurgitating and chewing the food stored in its stomach. Its master enlists someone else's help to unload the cargo from the camel's back. Slowly but surely the single prominent hump is revealed. There isn't any room for camels inside the Shorjah so their goods are dismantled a short distance away. From here the donkeys can finish the job.

A few yards further, an old model-T Ford with a tattered black cloth top is slowly brought to life by a man vigorously turning a crank at the front of it. After multiple attempts, the engine coughs, sputters and gurgles, all the while spewing out fumes from the rear.

A growing crowd of people are jostling their way down the narrow street, most carrying empty baskets made from palm fronds that will soon be overloaded with vegetables, fruit, and just about anything else. One has to pass with caution. Heavy electric cables, live wires, hang not too far from my very own window (when we were older, my mother told us that when my older brother was an infant, he grabbed a live wire and his fingers clenched before she could quickly yank him away).

Later in the morning I enjoy watching a man frying food in a small shop across the street. He is making lunches and snacks for shoppers on the run, an equivalent to present day fast food. Shish kabob was (and still is) typical fare. Yummy smells of grilled meat wafted upwards, smoke taking the shape of swirling mini-clouds.

My favorite store on our street - a large egg store – is owned by a Jewish man who was a family friend. We children were intrigued that he could tell exactly what was in each shell. It was almost as if he were clairvoyant. He knew if the eggs were fresh or if they contained double yolks. He would hold the egg in one hand, squint, and focus against the longitudinal axis of the egg toward the brightness of the outside as if he were inspecting a rare specimen through a microscope. We watched with reverence as he sorted through a large crate quickly and deftly, separating out the bad eggs and carefully arranging the good ones into neat layers cushioned by straw.

The best part for us was that he let us come into his store to play hide and seek among his many crates, each holding hundreds of eggs. Even better, in the summer time he stored his extra merchandise in the cool cellar of our house for a few days at a time. We didn't even have to leave home for our games! Looking back, those crates must have been incredibly sturdy. Otherwise it would have been like unleashing a stampede of bulls in a china shop.

When I grew older, I loved to accompany dad to the Shorjah for his morning grocery shopping. It was a pleasure for both father and son to spend this quality time together. The *souk* (market) was covered with corrugated iron sheets, dotted with holes admitting beams of sunlight and glistening particles of dust. It was cold in winter and very hot in summer. Vendors hoped to sell perishable goods for top prices early while they still looked appealing, for as the morning wore on, items wilted and fetched much lower prices.

Approaching the Shorjah, the din grows louder, the smells more intense and the crowds, well, more crowded. Bedouin women always come to the market early to sell breakfast to both vendors and shoppers. Clad in their black rough cloth *abayas*, they walk barefoot, balancing very high stacks of shallow round wooden containers filled with fresh yogurt on their heads.

Fresh produce can be placed on the ground in large wicker baskets or on the counters of crude stalls jammed close together in no particular order. There might be a fruit store next to a meat store. Spice stalls are the most colorful with mini-mountains of different colors. Across the way, a grain store houses large sacks of rice and wheat. A short distance to the left, a large heap of rose petals are laid on a large canvas.

Shoppers' baskets bulge with grapes, apricots, peaches, melons, lettuce, tomatoes, carrots, etc., depending on the season. We enjoy citrus fruits and apples in the autumn. Oranges are the biggest crop followed by sweet lemon, a fruit indigenous to Mesopotamia. It is the size of an orange with thin glistening skin. As its name implies, it is delightfully sweet but it turns bitter if bruised. For that reason isn't good for exporting. All the more to be enjoyed by us locals!

Dates are harvested in the summer. They come in many varieties. Price varied considerably depending on the type, ripeness or sweetness of the fruit. Some of the dates are allowed to stay on the trees until they are partially dry. Those could be stored for a long time and consumed in the winter months.

Dad and I weave our way through the rows of stalls, greeting this neighbor and picking fruit from that vendor. Eager to attract customers, the sellers hawk and sing out as to the superiority of *their* products, quality well above anyone else's. Once a buyer decides on something, he or she offers a price less than the asking one. Bargaining is common practice in the Mideast. The banter, raised voices and wild gesticulations are all part of the script illustrating a vital part of social communication. For those who have never witnessed such an exchange, it would seem that the two parties, buyer and seller, are arch enemies, ready to pull out their pistols and begin a duel. In most cases a price is finally reached. After all, the seller wants to sell, and the buyer wants to buy, although he has very likely threatened at least once to take his valuable business elsewhere if the seller doesn't propose a further price reduction. A handshake and a friendly slap on the back seals the deal and hints that these two will go at it again in the near future.

Not all shopping took place in the Shorjah. Sometimes my parents take me with them to the main shopping street in Baghdad, Al-Rashid Street. It is a wide and winding boulevard. There are sidewalks on each side, lined with classy shops and attractive display windows. This is the place to come to for good clothes, dry goods stores, shoemakers, tailors and the like. For me, these excursions aren't much fun. It is all too sedate and orderly. This area wasn't nearly as fun for a kid. The Shorjah is the *best* entertainment.

Old Baghdad

Top left: Tomb of Queen Zubaidah (died in July, 831), wife of Haroun Al-Rashid. She was the most famous Abbasid princess. She is best known for her water works – wells, man-made ponds and reservoirs – that served Muslim pilgrims on the route from Baghdad to Mecca and Medina. The story of the couple formed part of the tale for "The Thousand and One Nights."

Top right: Statue of King Faisal I (died 1933).

Bottom: Bridge over the Tigris River. On the right, the white house hosted government guests.

Part I

MY FAMILY'S PLACE IN BAGHDAD SOCIETY

My father's mother died in childbirth when he was 13 years old. She left Baruch, another son and 2 daughters. Several years later his father (my grandfather) told him that it was time for him to leave school and go to work. It wasn't that the family needed money. In those days there was no need to finish school. A boy should go out into the world and seek his fortune.

Work was hard to come by in those difficult years. Baruch heard that there were opportunities in India. Some two hundred years before a number of Iraqi Jews had settled there. He went to India and did not feel it was the place for him. He returned to Baghdad a couple of months later.

When Baruch was 28 he married Aliza, a woman half his age. It was common for women of all faiths to marry very young and start large families. Over the years they had 9 children, 6 boys and 3 girls. As years went by, Baruch became an enterprising businessman, a jack of all trades. His first venture was a joint one with his brother-in-law Aziz, who lived in Mosul. The two remained very close all their lives just as I have stayed very close to his son, my cousin Zaki. They set themselves up as a mini bank, transferring funds for clients between Baghdad and Mosul for a minimal charge. Over the years their business grew and they became wealthy.

My father, Baruch Shamash, early 1940s

At some point my father conjured up a woolen business. I remember this distinctly. He had workers shear lambs, wash the raw wool in the Tigris River and set it by the banks to dry in the sun. The fleece was dried, compressed and rolled up into large bales measuring approximately 3x4x3 feet and weighing about 200 pounds each. Such a bale was worth at least $500. They were shipped off to England to be woven into woolen textiles.

The export business soon turned into a two-way street, both exporting raw wool and importing finished British textiles. My father's half-brother, my Uncle Sion, went to London at the age of 19. He went into business shipping textiles and other British merchandise back to Baghdad to his father, his father's brother (my Uncle Selim) and my father too.

WWII made the shipping situation both long and perilous. Given the extent to which ships had to deviate from their course to avoid enemy attack, it could take many months for them to arrive with the goods. But Baruch knew his parcels would eventually materialize. He made deals "pre-selling" merchandise while it was still in transit. Money in hand, he would turn around and order more.

He joined into a partnership with a Muslim friend named Ahmed Abdul-Hamed. He and my father bought a large warehouse to store outbound wool and inbound finished goods (It was just the warehouse they shared. Mr. Abdul-Hamed was not involved in the woolen import/export business). Later on my father (on his own) bought another warehouse in a different part of Baghdad to store building material that he imported from America.

Along with the woolen import/export venture, father started investing in both residential and commercial real estate in

3

Baghdad. I'm not sure how much he ended up with, but it was a sizeable amount. Later on, the British were posted on farm land near the banks of the Tigris. When they left, the land was sold off. It changed hands once or twice before my father bought it. I remember the many glorious weekends we spent on that property as a family, enjoying our home away from home.

Soon the peace of Iraqi Jews was shattered. For two days, June 1st and 2nd of 1941, there was a disastrous event in Baghdad called the Farhud. It was a pogrom that took place during the Jewish holiday of *Shavout* (which celebrates the wheat harvest), not dissimilar to *Kristallnacht* ("the night of the broken glass") in Germany on November 9, 1938. I was a boy of 14. Hundreds of Jews were killed (I have seen numbers from 200-600). Many of them were buried in a mass grave. Thousands of people were injured. Women were raped. Jewish markets, homes and synagogues were destroyed.

Mr. Abdul-Hamed turned out to be a godsend. My father's partner, worried sick about us, walked almost 2 hours from his home in the eastern parts of Baghdad to come to our house. He arrived just in time, for within a half an hour, a soldier brandishing a rifle was banging furiously on the front door. Although our inner-city house was surrounded by a 10-foot high wall with a padlocked metal garden door, the soldier was hell-bent on getting through "to kill Jews." Mr. Abdul-Hamed, our angel from heaven, managed to talk him down. Eventually the soldier left, happy enough to take *baksheesh* (bribe) of about $120 with him. To this day, I remember our angel in my morning prayers!

It is a pity that he died many years later after an unsuccessful pacemaker operation when I, the son of his best friend, was implanting these devices frequently and successfully in the United States.

Some Members of My Family

Clockwise: my mother, Aliza with five children to date: Shaul, me, Maurice, Eliahou and Samra

Part II

1930s and early 1940s: My Youth

When I began my story, I was a young boy watching the throngs of people heading to the Shorjah from my balcony window in our first home. I was born in this house. Most people were born at home back then.

Birth certificates as we know them weren't issued on such occasions. A census was held every few years to take down the year someone was born, but no mention was made of a month or date. My father took his 3 eldest children (of which I was the third) to a mosque to "log us in." A man sat behind a wooden desk under an open sky. He asked, "How old is this one?" My father told him that the oldest was10, the next, 8, and finally me, 6. The man deducted our ages from the current year, say 1934, and record the birth year of the 3 children as 1924, 1926, and 1928 respectively. In my case, his recording was wrong. I knew full well that I was born on November 10, 1927.

The date of my birthday got a new twist many years later. Shortly before graduating from medical school, I purchased a

1950 two-door Chevy. When I applied for a driver's license, I wrote my birthday as 1928 in accordance with official papers. The man at the registry said I had to give him a month and a day in order for him to issue a license. No month or day had ever been noted. I arbitrarily picked the date of January 5, 1928, which I figured was close enough to the end of 1927. That date became my "official" birthday ever since.

For my first 89 years we celebrated my birthday as if I were born in 1928 even though I knew I wasn't. We celebrated it on the correct month and day, if not the right year! Finally, I told my family that in 2017 I would be celebrating my 90th birthday, not my 89th. We were spending a summer weekend together in our Cape Cod home when I dropped this bombshell. They just couldn't wrap their heads around the idea. I told them that I had indeed double-checked by calling my older brother, Eliahou, to ask him how old he was. He is exactly 2 years my senior.

All these years, and my kids had no idea. Nor did it make any sense to them. "Daddy, who wants to actually be a year OLDER than they really are, anyway?"

Well, I guess I do.

Our First House

Our house was situated on a corner of the very narrow alley where my "window cage" was located. The front door was a large black double door. A *mezuzah* was nailed to the inside frame on the right side. A *mezuzah* is a small encasement, usually made of ceramic or metal, containing a prayer inscribed on parchment. One is normally affixed to the door post of Jewish homes to remind us of our responsibilities and hopefully offer protection and good luck to those living within.

A large central courtyard sided with square yellow bricks and open to the sky greeted those entering our Baghdad home. Such courtyards are typical of hot climates. On the right side there was a large bathroom, a kitchen in the corner, and a stairway next to a covered porch. This porch was a wide room occupying the 2 sides open to the courtyard. The next corner and the third side had a few steps leading down to a cellar.

The cellar had a large well measuring approximately 8x12 feet. The well had several purposes. The family used it often to cool down in the summer. Although dry heat, temperatures easily rose above 110 degrees in July and August. We learned how to swim because the water was deep enough to cover a youngster's head. This pool had a Jewish ritual purpose as well. It served as *mikvah*, a bath used by both men and women, albeit separately, to achieve ritual purity for and after different occasions.

Back to the courtyard, the last corner contained a small room up a few steps where a large wooden swinging cradle hung from a decorative lathed wooden rod. That rod was in turn held by a pair of inverted Y-shaped lathed wooden supporters. This type of cradle was commonly used to soothe a crying child or sing an infant to sleep. The mother sat on the foot side of the cradle, giving her weary bones a rest.

Upstairs, 2 bedrooms faced the street. The large one was my parents' room. The beautiful furniture was part of my mother's trousseau. There was a large armoire and 3 beds: a small one in the corner, one for my father, and my mother's large bed with an exquisite brass headboard.

Every morning a brass samovar with coals was fired up to heat the flange holding the tea pot. Our favorite drink was hot milk mixed with tea and sugar. We drank it from a small glass with a narrow waist, always less than full so it could be held with the fingers from the top part without getting burned.

Two or 3 small children, me included, shared my mother's bed. It was next to a large window facing the small side street. When I was very young I remember how I tried to squeeze as close to the window as possible so I could crane my neck and look outside to see what was happening in the street below. Many a night, I woke up in the early morning hours wet and cold. How could I have wet the bed and not known! I'd get a firm scolding and was told not to do it again.

I watched mother diapering the baby by carefully and firmly wrapping the tiny thing in a small home-made triangular sheet. She straightened each limb until the infant was stiff as a papoose, it was swaddled so tight. All I could see was the little head poking out. I begged to hold the infant in my lap after it was fed (there was no milk formula in those days. Children were breast fed until the age of 9 months).

Adjacent to the bedroom side there was a covered porch. The third side had a drawing room. There was also a moderate-sized attic in the corner, which could be used as an extra bedroom. There were no rooms on the fourth side of the house that bordered the narrow alleyway. A small half bath was in the corner next to the 2 front bedrooms.

More stairs led up to the flat roof which was covered by floor bricks and surrounded by a wall that bordered the outside perimeter of the house. On the opposite side, the courtyard side, there was a protective railing. The family slept on the roof under the stars and a beautiful moon during the 3 hottest summer months. Thankfully there was no rain this time of year. It would have been unbearably hot to sleep inside. Every morning, the bedding had to be put into a small alcove at the top of the stairs to keep it out of the grueling sun. It was brought back out to the roof after sunset along with a large, porous jug filled with water. Evaporation from the outer walls of the jug kept the water cool enough to quench thirst during the hot nights. We woke up in the mornings to a very pleasant temperature with crisp air and clear sunrise.

Like most well-to-do families, we had help. There was a live-in maid who barely spoke Arabic. Like most of the help in Baghdad, she came from the Kurdish part of the country in the north. She got room and board and a bit of money for her services.

Once a week, a professional clothes–washer arrived early in the morning and spent all day. She heated water and poured it into a couple of large round copper basins measuring approximately 3-1/2 feet in diameter by 8 inches deep. The clothes were left to soak in one of them for a while. When the linens were ready to be dealt with, the lady sat on a small, low wooden stool. She took one piece of clothing at a time from the soaking basin, moved it to the next one and scrubbed it in the sudsy hot water. She used special irregular white bars of locally produced soap, different from the greenish-brown soap we used for bathing. By the afternoon, the clothes were brought up to the top of the flat roof and strung out on clotheslines to dry in the baking sun.

This washing activity took up all the space in the not-so-large open courtyard of the house. When our private playground was pre-empted by the "washing lady," we had to find somewhere else to play. The best bet was going down to the basement and playing hide-and-seek among the huge crates from the egg man's store.

We didn't have a cook. My mother did the cooking. I especially remember the meals she made for the *Shabbat*. On my way to school Friday mornings, dad and I would stop at the market and purchase a live chicken, making sure it was big enough to feed all of us. Then we took it to a particular person who could slaughter it in keeping with *kashrut*, the rules of Jewish dietary law. After school I picked up the chicken and brought it home to my mother.

She plucked all the feathers by hand. Then she lit a match to a newspaper and put the whole chicken over the fire to get rid of all the feather roots. She proceeded to wash and salt it before hanging it over the sink for 2 hours or so. She cooked it in a pot with all kinds of vegetables and condiments. She filled the upside-down cover with a dozen eggs. The chicken pot was placed over burning coals that were covered with heavy rags to keep the fire minimal. It cooked slowly overnight. On Saturday morning we ate the nicely browned eggs when we returned from temple services. That evening we feasted on the still warm chicken for *Shabbat* dinner.

Backing up to Friday night, we ushered in the Sabbath by saying *Kiddush,* a blessing recited over wine or grape juice to sanctify the holiday. We used dried black grapes to make juice. Mother made a dish called *kibbe*. She cooked handfuls of rice, beat it to form a dough-like consistency and filled it with ground meat. Some 20 such *kibbes* were placed in a large pot with vegetables and cut-up tomatoes and cooked for a few hours.

Accidents, Sickness and the Doctor

During my childhood, I suffered the usual knocks and bruises of a boy at play. One afternoon my brother and I were horsing around in the house. I was only about 4 years old, but I remember this incident vividly. He was chasing me, so I scurried up the few stairs to the small room in the corner of the house where we put the cradle. I held on to the edge of the next step, and in my haste my forehead struck forcefully against the sharp wooden edge. The next thing I knew, blood was pouring down my face from a huge gash. My frightened mother held a towel firmly against my forehead. I could sense that she was very nervous because tears came to her eyes. I told her over and over that I was OK and it didn't hurt.

Disregarding all that I had said, she whisked me off to the doctor's office on Rashid Street, Baghdad's main street. It was a good 15 minute walk from the house and she was absolutely frantic. As we scurried she did her best to keep the bloody towel pressed to my forehead.

Her hysteria melted away once we got to the doctor's office. Dr. Raouf was a young good-looking man with a soothing voice. He came from the city of Mosul in the north of Iraq, where my father had many relatives. He was actually a distant relative of my father's brother-in-law and business partner, Aziz. Aside from private practice, he worked in the Baghdad medical school and hospital. He held the respect of his peers and of my father, who chose him as our family physician.

He reassured my mother, left her in his waiting room and escorted me into a room which smelled strongly of some sterile odor. I lay down, and after the sting of a pinprick, I felt no more pain. I followed the doctor's hands moving rhythmically back and forth over my face as he stitched up the "cut." The motion was hypnotic and I was mesmerized.

In no time, mother and I we were on our way, walking through the *souk* toward home. Once healed, I returned to the doctor's office to have the metal suture removed. I was surprised to see that it was a single thin piece of curled wire that held my injured face together, implemented by a man who spent his career helping people.

On occasion the doctor was invited to our house in the evening for a cocktail. The whole family gathered together in our drawing room. My father would ask me to sing something I learned in kindergarten, like *Karem ha-Yeladim* (Vineyard of Children), both the name of the song and the name of the school). Our guest would clap to show his approval of my performance. This handsome doctor impressed me with his consideration, gentle manner and expertise in his work. He was my role model, motivating me years later to seek a future in medicine.

I was 14 when we left my first house. By now my mother had 7 of her 9 children. At the age of 14, she was taken out of school and put on to the *bimah* (altar) for marriage, the matchmaker having made her a match. She had her first child, my brother Shaul, in 1924 and her ninth, David, 20 years later.

Our Second Home

In the summer of 1940 we moved from the old city of Baghdad to a suburban area on Sa'doun St. We had plenty of help, even more than we had in the last house. We had a live-in gardener, a Muslim woman who milked our cow, and 2 other helpers. One was in charge of cooking and cleaning and the other took care of all the kids.

Our large house sat on a double lot, 60 meters frontage with 30 meters in depth. An 8-foot high metal gate and a 10-foot brick wall surrounded the perimeter of the property. One entered on to a brick terrace and walked around the front of the house to enter through the garden. A small wooden lattice scaffold covered with green vines led to a brick path flanked on both sides by wide beds of annual flowers. The path outlined the large rectangular green lawn in the center and came out again to the back end of the brick terrace. On the outside of this path a row of beautiful orange and lemon trees lined the inside of the surrounding wall.

Once a week our gardens were irrigated with untreated water from the Tigris River, stored in a small trench in the street. Each house had a large pipe that connected from that trench to a smaller trench inside the yard. The lawn, citrus trees and flower beds were flooded with about 3 inches of water, enough to last until the process was repeated in a week's time.

Having lived in the inner city, it was such a pleasure for me and the rest of my siblings to walk barefoot on the soft cool lawn during summertime. We came back from school about 2pm and had lunch, the main meal of the day. Then we retired to a cool part of the house for a short rest before going back outside. In the late afternoon I enjoyed doing yard work, watering the flowers with the hose or pushing the lawnmower.

Having a beautiful garden nourished by water from the Tigris wasn't always a blessing. In the second or third year after moving into this house and spending more and more time on the lawn, I noticed that my urine showed a pink tinge and at times a few drops of thin blood. At first, I didn't know what to make of this.

I was already in my third year of high school and our biology class textbook covered things like venereal disease and parasitic infections indigenous to the Middle East. As a teenager just passing through puberty, many thoughts crossed my mind, none of which seemed too healthy to me. Could this be a venereal disease? According to the primitive description in our biology book, the results of such an illness could go beyond merely unpleasant and inconvenient to death at an early age. I kept this bad news from my parents and siblings.

A few months later we studied a disease spread by contact with fresh water containing parasites - parasites that produced blood in the urine. I wasn't suffering from venereal disease after all! I could live to old age. However, this new thing from which I certainly *did* suffer was no less pleasant. It was called bilharzia, probably named for the person who discovered the illness and the parasite. It is also called schistosomiasis.[3]

During a brief period in the life cycle of this parasite it takes the form of a small worm that entered the body via cracks in the skin, usually between the toes. It traveled through the blood stream and finally settled in the urinary bladder, causing bleeding in the urine. Our text book, which might have been outdated even for the early 1940s, stated that there was no specific cure for this malady. It usually affected farmers in the Middle East, resulting in death after a certain number of years.

Again, I said nothing to my parents. Mother, with 9 children to care for, was surely too busy for this news. My father was engrossed in his work. When he left the office it was time to relax together, tell stories and have fun. I told myself, "Why bother anyone when this was not a treatable disease anyway?" I would

---

[3] **Schistosomiasis**, also known as snail fever and bilharzia, is a disease caused by parasitic flatworms called schistosomes. The urinary tract or the intestines may be infected. Symptoms include abdominal pain, diarrhea, bloody stool, or blood in the urine. Those who have been infected for a long time may experience liver damage, kidney failure, infertility, or bladder cancer. In children, it may cause poor growth and learning difficulty. The disease is spread by contact with fresh water contaminated with the parasites. These parasites are released from infected freshwater snails. The disease is especially common among children in developing countries as they are more likely to play in contaminated water. Other high risk groups include farmers, fishermen, and people using unclean water during daily living.

https://en.wikipedia.org/wiki/Schistosomiasis

be gone soon, a life cut much too short. There seemed no point in disturbing everyone for nothing. The inevitable would happen in due time.

Sooner rather than later, my observant mother noticed bloodstains on my underwear. She inquired; I told her my story and informed her that nothing could be done. She promptly took me to Dr. Raouf once again. He tested my urine for parasites, found the offending culprit and prescribed a series of injections. These shots, jabbed deep into my buttock muscles once a week for several weeks, were extremely painful. I was told it might cause lightheadedness, and to be careful walking home.

I later learned that the parasite contained a heavy metal antimony that was imported from Germany.[4] Eventually my urine became clear and I learned my lesson not to walk barefoot on the lawn. A few years later, one of my younger brothers caught the same illness and he was treated in the same way.

Schools

My entire school experience in Baghdad was wonderful. Although public schools were very good, the Jewish community

---

[4] *Antimony* is a semi metallic chemical element which can exist in two forms: the metallic form is bright, silvery, hard and brittle; the nonmetallic form is a grey powder. Human exposure to antimony can take place by breathing air, drinking water and eating foods that contain it, but also by skin contact with soil, water and other substances that contain it. As the exposure continues more serious health effects may occur, such as lung diseases, heart problems, diarrhea, severe vomiting and stomach ulcers.

https://www.lenntech.com/periodic/elements/sb.htm#ixzz4wYXyUdX9

funded their own schools through the Jewish Federation and took great pride in them as the best. I remember that my pre-school, *Karem ha-Yeladim* (Vineyard of Children) was a lot of fun, filled with songs and laughter.

At the age of 5 I started kindergarten, which was part of primary school. My father took me every morning. I held his right forefinger in my left hand, trying hard to keep up with his strident gait. We cut through the Shorjah market. At the end of it we took a right turn, went through some narrow streets and finally arrived at the Rahel Shahmoon School.

Rahel Shahmoon was a local woman who died from an illness within a week after she was married. Her father used her dowry and provided additional funds to build a school in her memory. It was established in 1923. It was a big two-storey structure with two large open courtyards and multiple rooms for each of the grades. The younger children shared the smaller courtyard, and the older ones, the larger courtyard. Seen through the eyes of a 5-year-old I'm sure that the building seemed even more gigantic than it was. The sun shone on the brick and poured through the large glass windows of each room. It was a very bright and airy space, filled with the new crop of youngsters who were playing, singing and learning to read and write.

In first grade, I had a heady experience. One Friday morning before the first bell, an older student asked me to help him with reading to better prepare him for an upcoming quiz. I obliged, and in return he gave me one *fils* (one thousand *fils* made a *dinar*, equivalent to $4 in 1930s). I was especially glad to get the stipend because every Friday it was customary for us children to put a donation into the *tzedakah* (charity) box. Today I forgot to bring money from home. I was proud that for the first time, "little me" could be of help to others with money I earned.

We studied 3 languages in primary school. We worked on improving reading and writing in Arabic, our native language. Hebrew was taught only once a week. English was much harder. We began learning it in third grade and continued with it for the rest of our education. Many hours were spent diligently writing the letters of the alphabet neatly between lines, copying each letter from a printed top line. We were graded on our work so we took this in earnest.

I did much better in languages that year than math. I just didn't understand division and I flunked. That killed the next summer. I had to take a make-up class to prepare for an exam. If and *only* if I passed it could I advance to the next grade.

Our principal was a strict man with limited eyesight. He could see well enough to walk around the school and check on the teachers and students. His name was Shim-oon. Instead of calling him "Principal Shim-oon," as is done in the U.S., we called him "Shim-oon Effendi." "Effendi" means principal, and in Arabic, it comes after the name.

Shim-oon Effendi liked to teach math. When he came into the classroom, unannounced, everyone jumped to attention. He motioned for us to sit. Then he proceeded to teach fractions.

"Take an orange and assume that it has 10 pieces. If you take 2 pieces.... " He would go to blackboard and feel for the chalk and eraser by running his hands over the narrow trough at the bottom. His thick, red meaty hands became covered in white dust. He wrote the number 2 on the board, drew a horizontal line under it and put the number 10 below the line. He continued this process for a good half-hour, writing different portion amounts of the orange slices over the top of the horizontal line, and with the "whole" of the orange below this line. Sure enough, our principal drove the concept of fractions into our brains. Upon completion of his presentation, he put the dusty eraser and chalk down. He clapped his large, now-white meaty palms with gusto, sending a white cloud directly to his face. This loud clap was his signature, forever to be imprinted in our minds.

Discipline was meted out swiftly and painfully. If we didn't behave, we'd find ourselves on the receiving end of his massive hands. Still, we knew deep down that underneath his strict façade was a warm and caring heart. He had long since gained the trust and affection of parents, teachers and students.

By the fourth grade and beyond we had gym classes regularly. They were held in the courtyard during mid-session or toward the end of the day. We mimicked the teacher as he jumped, arms extended up, down and sideways. Most of us enjoyed gym, but as a group we weren't athletically-inclined.

At the age of 10 we were eligible to join the Boy Scouts. I loved my uniform. We wore a small green scarf around the neck and a *sidara* (hat) with an insignia on the front. Joining the Scouts made us all feel like good citizens showing allegiance to our country. The highlight was our field trip to the annual citywide gymnastics forum run by the Ministry of Education. It showcased the top athletes chosen from all the Baghdad schools. We sat with

Sisters Rachele (left) and Samra stand on the veranda of our new yellow brick suburban home.

Wearing my Boy Scout uniform, age 10

our gym teacher on the edge of a large field watching the stars compete in the high jump, disc-throwing and other events.

There were a couple of excellent Jewish secondary schools in Baghdad. The older boys in my family, including me, attended the Shamash School (no relation). It was built by a family at the turn of the century who eventually emigrated to England. The school had the reputation of being the best secondary school in Iraq. We had British faculty members and English text books from which we learned algebra, trigonometry, physics and chemistry.

Although most of the students were Jewish, it was open to all qualified students. Our class had an Arab female student from a well-to-do family. She was somewhat shy, courteous and a good student. Her family must have thought that she would get a superior education attending our school.

The Shamash School prepared its students for 2 crucial exams. One was the National Secondary School Exam given every year by the Ministry of Education. Upon successful completion the student got a proper diploma. The second was the matriculation examinations of the University of London, administered at the British Consulate every January. Five subjects were covered over a 3-day period. In January of 1945, I passed this exam in English, Arabic, arithmetic, chemistry and physics.

Instead of the Shamash School, my younger siblings attended the French Alliance Israelite School. It was begun by French Jews to educate Jewish communities in the Arab countries. The benefit of this school was learning French which was not taught at the Shamash School. It included grades from kindergarten to intermediate, a total of 9 years, short only of the last 2 years needed to finish secondary school. At that point, my siblings as well as others came to the Shamash School to be prepared for the 2 exams previously mentioned.

My First Experience with Death

One late Friday afternoon, a short time before the onset of *Shabbat,* a frightening cry shattered the stillness in our home. The wailing shrieks went on for a few agonizing minutes. They were was coming from a neighbor's house to the rear.

The mother of the household had been standing on a chair to clean and dust some furniture near an upstairs open window. She lost her balance, fell out of the window, landed on the courtyard bricks and died instantly. It was her teenage girls who were screaming those piercing sounds. Needless to say, our household was very saddened that evening. I couldn't sleep alone that night. My older brother and I hugged each other tightly before we fell asleep together.

The next morning was Saturday and therefore *Shabbat.* Jewish holidays always start and end at sundown. *Shabbat* starts Friday at sundown and ends on Saturday at sundown. We were told that a dead person could not be moved from his/her position on the *Shabbat* – until a loaf of bread was placed on the deceased.

This sounds quite strange, so I'll explain. Orthodox Jews aren't permitted to do any work on *Shabbat.* Moving something, including a dead body, is considered work. If, however, one saw some bread on the floor, one would be obliged to pick it up. So if the bread was placed *onto* the deceased, the bread, along with the body, would have to be picked up. No work would be involved.

Jewish burials normally take place as quickly as possible because bodies are not embalmed. Burial can't take place on *Shabbat*, so if one dies on a Friday, as my neighbor did, burial couldn't take place before Saturday sundown. That is when the crowd gathered. Chanting psalms, we carried our neighbor to the cemetery.

Many times on the way to or from school I saw masses of people carrying a dead person to his last repose. It was common for passersby to join the procession because it was considered a good deed in general and a tribute to the deceased. There was no obituary page in the newspapers. Communication of such news occurred by word of mouth via coffee houses or through local synagogues.

Religion: Celebrations and Synagogues

Judaism played a big part in our everyday lives and there was nothing more wonderful than celebrating a holiday or a special event. I remember one well: Passover of 1939.

We gathered around the Seder table, beautifully decorated with an embroidered white tablecloth. Certain ritual foods were laid out on the table: *matzos*, eggs, bitter herbs, parsley, lettuce and lamb shank. Everyone had a wine cup. After our self-conducted service we enjoyed a smorgasbord of rice, peas, chicken, meat, etc.

The whole family participated in reading and singing the passages of the *Haggadah* (text for the Passover Seder) both in Hebrew and Arabic, relating the story of the exodus of the Hebrews from Egypt. We enumerated the 10 plagues one by one. For each plague my father poured one drop of wine into a small dish. The contents of that dish symbolically contained all the evil tortures that the Lord inflicted on the Egyptians because their Pharaoh didn't follow his command: "Let my people go!" That tainted wine was not to be drunk. I waited for my father to signal me with a glance from the corner of his eye. That was my cue to remove the dish and pour the wine down the toilet.

Returning back to the Seder table, we continued chanting in unison. We celebrated the Lord's parting of the Red Sea which let our people flee from Egypt. The Pharaoh's army with horses and chariots followed them in hot pursuit. Alas, they couldn't recapture their victims. The Lord retaliated by unleashing the sea waters, drowning and sinking the whole lot of them. We sang the song of Miriam, Moses' sister, as she beheld the sight of the deluge.

Then we gave thanks to God for sustaining us over those 40 years in the desert. He gave us Manna from heaven as well as food for the soul: his Ten Commandments, the Torah, and the Sabbath. Throughout the service we reiterated that it wasn't just our forefathers who were redeemed, but us as well. If they hadn't been rescued, we wouldn't be here today.

Then it was time for us kids to seek the *afikoman* and get a present. The *afikoman* is part of a piece of *matzos* (unleavened bread) that was split earlier in the evening in a shape that resembles the parting of the Red Sea. Our father wrapped the *afikoman* in a cloth napkin and hid it somewhere when he thought we were too busy eating our dinner to notice. He usually put it behind some pillow in the corner of the room. I kept a keen eye to make sure I knew exactly where it was stowed.

After dinner but before dessert, my father asked if one of us kids could find it. I would quickly retrieve it, and with a big smile demand a "price" for it. This could be a piece of silver money or some present. I loved winning the prize. After the late evening I went to bed tired but elated, having shared the story of our past, a terrific meal, and best of all, winning a present.

There was a reason that I remember this particular Passover so well. The next morning the newspaper headlines shocked us all. King Ghazi, son of King Faisal, was killed when he lost control of his convertible and struck a steel lamp post in the median of the road during the night. He had ruled Iraq since 1933. It was as if the whole country shut down. Schools and businesses were closed. Streets, balconies and roofs were full of people trying to catch a glimpse of the funeral procession. I remember going with my mother to her father's house where we watched the procession from the roof. The panoply took hours, or at least it seemed that way to me. The air was filled with sadness in Baghdad that day, for Ghazi was loved by his people.

In the fall of 1941 I had my bar mitzvah, my coming of age as a Jewish man. Family and friends gathered in our large living room on a Thursday afternoon. This formal room off of the foyer with its own door was used primarily for receiving guests. The family normally used another informal sitting room.

I wore my new *tallit* (prayer shawl). As part of the ceremony, my maternal grandfather, Moshe, stood next to me and showed me how to wear my new *tefillin*. Also called phylacteries from the ancient Greek, *tefillin* are small black leather boxes containing scrolls of parchment inscribed with text from the Torah. One box is placed on the upper arm, and the other, above the forehead. They are worn by men when they pray.

The text on the scrolls contains this message: "and these words that I am instructing you today be placed in your heart, and you should diligently teach them to your children and instruct them while you sit down in your home, and while you walk with them on the street, and while you recline and while you get up, and you should bind them as a sign on your arm and between your eyes, and you should write them on your door posts and in your dwellings."

After reciting the proper blessings, my grandfather unraveled a long black leather strip. He carefully applied one of the boxes to the middle of my left upper arm and wrapped the long leather strip down the arm to my hand. He placed the second square leather compartment, mounted on another circular leather strip just above my forehead. We recited prayers together: "Hear O' Israel - the Lord our God, the Lord is ONE." When we finished, he showed me how to remove the *tefillin* properly, winding up the long leather strips. My mother sewed a pouch to store these precious items. I recognized the material, a sample of imported Indian cloth I had seen in my father's office.

At the conclusion of the prayers, the female contingent sang the customary ululations - shrieking sounds produced by quick vibrations of the vocal cords and tongue in combination. This indicates satisfaction and pleasure. For those who have never heard such sounds, they would be considered quite strange indeed. Guests were offered *arak* to drink. It's somewhat similar to vodka but made from dates. Everyone socialized and had a good time. Within about an hour or so, they went home.

My grandfather told me that every morning I should take my *tefillin* and go to synagogue with my older brother for morning prayers. We left for the Meir Taweig Synagogue at about 6am, returned home for breakfast at 7am, and headed to school by 8am. I kept up this daily routine until my departure from Baghdad on July 9, 1947.

Our Synagogues in Baghdad

On Saturday mornings the whole family went to synagogue together. The men sat downstairs on upholstered wooden sofas. The women sat upstairs in the balcony overlooking the main floor of the sanctuary. The *bimah* (altar), a carved wooden platform elevated off the floor, was located in the center of the sanctuary. This is where the rabbi, cantor and community leaders sat. Special cabinets in the wall formed the ark that housed the torah scrolls. The ark doors were usually kept open throughout the services on Saturdays and special holidays, rather than alternately opening and closing them as is the custom in other countries. At the completion of services, the women came down from the balcony

I have put on my *tallit* and *tefillin* to pray almost every morning since my bar mitzvah. My left arm is wrapped with one leather strip. The other strip circles my head with the small black box containing the scripture.

and lined up to approach the *bimah*. They kissed the outer case of the Torah and moved their lips in silent prayer.

There were probably as many as 50 synagogues in all of Baghdad. In my early childhood, when we lived near the Shorjah in the old city, my older brother and I went to the nearby "Great Synagogue" of Baghdad. It was approximately 850 years old. To me it certainly *looked* very old. Two or 3 sides of the building had large chambers facing a central open courtyard. Each chamber had a dome-shaped ceiling made of brick. They were similar in shape to the domes at some of the mosques, but without any ornamentation or color.

On holidays my father took us to the Alliance School, which had a beautiful paneled sanctuary. On the High Holidays they set up seats in the school's large courtyard. Huge sheets of canvas were strung from one side of the second floor balcony to the other, shading the courtyard below. Even in early fall the sun could be hot and annoying. I remember these services vividly as a young child. The congregation kept the tots happy by passing out special sweet biscuits that looked like bagels.

The Shamash School had a synagogue on the first floor. We saw the men leaving it as we arrived to start our classes. In my last couple of years there, from 1943-1945, we had a chemistry teacher who came from Eastern Europe. I observed him praying fervently. He swayed forward and backward, lips moving without any audible sound, eyes frequently closed. He was a good teacher and always very serious. Retrospectively I often wondered if he had relatives in Europe during the war who suffered from atrocities at the hand of Hitler.

Some Members of My Family

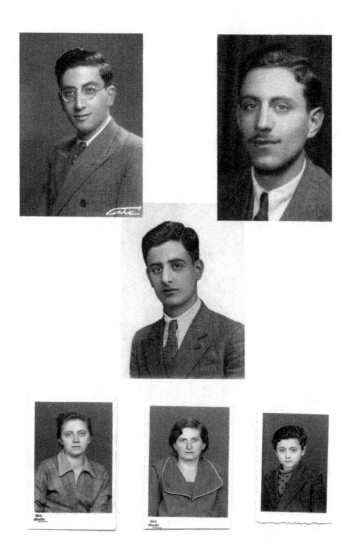

Caption: From left to right, top row: The 3 oldest in order: Shaul, Eliahou, and me

Bottom row, left to right: Rachele, my mother, Aliza, and David, the youngest

Part III

LEAVING BAGHDAD

After finishing secondary school I didn't have concrete plans for my future, though deep in my heart, I knew I wanted to become a doctor and help other people. One applied after secondary school, unlike in the United States, where one attends college first. Medical school lasted 6 or 7 years since it included college. Baghdad Medical College enrolled just 40 new students each year. Out of the 40 they only took 2 to 4 Jewish students. They really knew how to let us know that we weren't favored. One year, student interviews were held on *Yom Kippur*, the Jewish annual fast day and holiest day of the year. A large *baksheesh* (bribe), thousands of dollars, would have to be paid by my father to give me even the slightest chance of an acceptance. That is the way things were done. Needless to say, I decided to skip applying to our local medical school.

In the fall of 1945 and into 1946 I applied to medical schools in England. Meanwhile, I enrolled in a post-graduate 2-year night school program in business at our Shamash School. There I sharpened my skills in bookkeeping, accounting, and economics. At the same time I began correspondence courses in English and mathematics with the Hebrew University in Jerusalem. The English course stressed grammar and short essay-writing.

As I reflect now, it was nothing short of a miracle for me to have sent and received mail from Palestine and especially a Hebrew institution in those times without any censorship. Anti-Zionist sentiments were coming to a boil in Iraq. To be labeled a Zionist meant jail or much worse. In later years those innocent people were hanged. This happened to a rich Jew from the southern city of Basra who had the sole auto dealerships for Ford and GM. Such actions by the dictatorial regime were jealous and vengeful hatred gone amok against people who did nothing to deserve them.

In January of 1945 I sat for the matriculation examination of the University of London. The exams were administered at the British Consulate. The exam papers arrived in sealed packages from London and were opened only after we were all seated and were ready to take the test. Most of the tests required answers to 3 out of 4 questions, which allowed one a better chance to choose familiar material. It was a rigorous 3-day series of 5 examinations, 2 hours each, in English, algebra, physics, chemistry and Arabic.

The morning of the first exam I was smacked with a wave of nausea. I felt unprepared and inadequate. I couldn't eat my simple breakfast of milk-and-tea, cheese and bread. I felt so light-headed and sick to my stomach on my way out the front door that I lay down on the path. I broke out into a sweat and started heaving. All that came out was a small amount of very bitter-tasting bile. Then I felt much better. My mother told me, "You will do fine! Have faith." Heeding her advice, I got up and marched forward. I would give it my best shot and accept the outcome, whatever it may be.

Within a few months I received the result. The certificate read, "It is with pleasure to inform you that you have successfully passed the requirement of the matriculation examination of the University of London," signed "I remain your obedient servant" so-and-so. I was very proud indeed! Once accepted, I went to the British Consulate across the Tigris River in West Baghdad. As part of my visa application I had to write a short account of what I would be doing in England during my stay there.

I signed my name for the first time in English at the bottom of the page with two of the letter "m," writing Shammash instead of Shamash. By the way it sounded in Arabic I thought it should be written "my" way. Since that time I am the only member of my family who spells our name with a double "m." I felt a sense of accomplishment to have done all of this on my own.

My attempts at applying to British medical schools were not successful. The response of the various schools was the same: British subjects returning from the war would have priority over foreign applicants. Some of the schools suggested applying to Indian medical schools, stressing that they were of high standards. I applied to some of them and was amazed at the length and complexity of the application forms. They were certainly more involved than those of their British counterparts.

I decided to switch gears and seek entry into engineering schools. In 1946 I was accepted to Loughborough College in Leicestershire, England. Shortly thereafter I applied for an Iraqi passport and a visa to study in the U.K. It took me about 3 months to get my passport. With persistence and patience, I waited for hours outside some clerk's office only to be told to come back tomorrow or the next week. I was pleased that I accomplished the whole process successfully without paying any *baksheesh* to the clerks.

I continued to prepare for my trip to England. Discussing my plan with friends and family, I discovered that almost everything was still being rationed in England, including basics like tea, coffee and sugar. I was advised to go to the United States, where living standards were starting to rise post-war and where most rationing restrictions had ended by 1945. That sounded like a better idea. I filled out application forms for The Massachusetts Institute of Technology (MIT), New York University and Harvard. The replies were similar to the ones I received from England. Places were reserved for GI's returning from the war.

MIT was part of a consortium of about 10 liberal arts colleges. They couldn't take me right away. They suggested I start by spending 3 years at another one of those associated schools. Then I could transfer to MIT for the final 2 years. I would finish with 2 degrees, a B.A. from the first college and B.S. from MIT.

I applied to Middlebury College (Vermont) in 1946 and was accepted. They asked if I could defer entry to September of 1947. All sorted! I put the tune of "Rule, Britannia!" out of my head and looked forward to meeting the Statue of Liberty.

Now that I had already gone through the rigmarole of getting my passport and student visa for the U.K., I needed to get one for the U.S.A. This process was no snap either. I had to fill out a long form, get a chest X-ray and be examined by a United States-approved physician. Then I would have an interview with Mr. King at the American Consulate. He asked why I wanted to travel to his country and whether I intended to remain in the U.S. I told him that I just wanted a student visa. I knew that a permanent visa was definitely out of the question. Iraq only allowed 50 people a year to emigrate out of one thousand applicants. It was music to my ears when Mr. King told me to have a wonderful time at Middlebury.

It was a warm, clear afternoon on the 9th of July, 1947. Today was the day I would leave my home to further my studies. I had no idea that I would never return.

The previous week I started gathering my bits and pieces of memorabilia and credentials that I wanted to bring: books, diplomas, my secondary school grades, letter of recommendation from the principal and the certificate from London University. My United States student visa, issued a couple of months earlier after my brief interview with Mr. Bayard King, was in a separate large envelope stamped with United States seal. Next to this I held my Iraqi passport with the exit visa. The third document was an affidavit issued by the Iraqi CID (equivalent to the CIA), stating that I was *not* allowed passage to Palestine. If I were to disobey this decree, my father would have to pay the Iraqi Government ID 2000 (about $8,000).

Along with my treasured bundle of papers I took the $900 in cash that my father gave me for my tuition and expenses. I carefully placed it behind a book cover and wrapped the package securely, binding it with tape. I put a few articles of clothing, including my best suit, into an old cardboard suitcase. As I packed my mother would say, "How about this sweater or that shirt?" I kept repeating, "There is no more room! The suitcase won't close." She was having a really tough time with my departure. Her eyes brimmed with tears. "You're going so far away. You won't come back." I told her not to worry, and promised that when I finished my studies I would be eager to return home.

Leaving Baghdad
July 9, 1947

Everyone gathered to bid me farewell. Top, left to right: Aunt Esther, Shaul, me, cousin Haron, Samra, Maurice, cousin Yas, Eliahou Sha'shua (Haron's brother, not to be confused with my brother Eliahou. Bottom: In front of my bus. Left to right: Maurice, me and Samra.

My parents and eight siblings dressed up for pictures and gathered in our beautiful garden. I held my baby brother David, only 2-1/2 years old. At about 2pm we all left the house. We crossed the Tigris River to reach the outdoor terminal of the special bus, Nairon, run by Thomas Cook. My journey would begin with an overnight trip across the desert to Syria. We hugged, received more family, took more pictures and said our goodbyes. My mother's eyes streamed with tears, my siblings shouted "Good luck!", and my father offered reassuring glances that said "You'll do just fine." I looked back at all of them for just one moment. With trepidation, I climbed up into the massive bus.

The décor was plush, fresh white linen covering the wide seats. I sank into my seat, took a deep breath and began to relax in the cool air. Soon we were on our way across the western desert. The setting sun washed its golden rays against the brown desert floor. Soon it was gone. I closed my eyes and reluctantly said goodbye to my birthplace.

The next morning we arrived at a clean but simple structure at the edge of the desert marking the border of Syria. Breakfast, the usual milk-and-tea and yogurt, tasted delicious. The rising sun, a red-hot copper disk, was a marvel to behold. After few hours we reached Syrian customs. We paid a significant sum for the obligatory transit visa. At least we had a souvenir of the stamp in our passport to show for it.

Onward to Lebanon! The bus navigated a serpentine path upward through the hilly terrain to a small village. Many city dwellers fled to the cooler hills when the work week was done.

There I joined my uncle Selim and his family, on holiday from London, for a few restful days.

When I left Baghdad I didn't have a ship booking because Thomas Cook didn't have any vacancies. I was advised me to get to Beirut well ahead of any scheduled departure in the event they had cancellations. I was traveling with another student headed to Lafayette College in Pennsylvania. Upon arrival in mid-July we enjoyed many a day hiking some of the low hills in the outskirts of Beirut. We delighted in the cool climate and marveled at the occasional picturesque waterfall cascading down rugged edges of stone. We took pictures to document our pleasant experience and mail to our families. Our entire journey was filled with sightseeing, photos, adventure and pure fun.

We soon received word from our parents that Thomas Cook expected a ship in a few days bound for New York. We left the hills for the city to wait for it. Beirut was a beautiful, clean town. Rolling hills were scattered with villas and colorful gardens set against a background of olive trees. Opposite, the deep blue expanse of the Mediterranean stretched as far as the eye could see. A few ships were anchored in the harbor, but ours was yet to arrive. We spent a couple of nights in a small hotel. One afternoon we had lunch in an outdoor café on the edge of the sea. One could stand up, look straight down into the water and spot the occasional fish wiggling and searching for food as we waited to be served ours. The gentle breeze made ripples in the water reflecting prismatic spectrums of color.

At long last, our (retired war) ship sailed in. The *Marine Carp* was a Type C4 class ship, the largest cargo ships built by the United States Maritime Commission (MARCOM) during WWII. Originally intended for the American-Hawaiian Lines, her design plans were taken over late in 1941 by the MARCOM. The *Marine Carp* was one of 81 troopships built in 4 shipyards around the United States. Now that she had finished moving troops, she was moving people like me. She stood before us, securely anchored by the loading dock at the harbor. This tall, massive structure dressed in shabby gray-black and sporting multiple decks would be home for the next 16 days.

After our passports and visas were checked, we were issued a "luggage tag," a large red, white and blue sticker on which to write our name and destination. A prominent letter B indicated the level of our deck. After affixing the stickers, the passengers' luggage was assembled together at the foot of the long ramp. My friend and I proudly ascended and the luggage followed suit. Leaning against the railing, we watched the hustle and bustle below as the moorings were unhitched and the ship slipped away from land. Beirut sparkled under the setting sun. Soon enough the buildings dissolved into tall shadows and shapeless forms.

We went down to the cafeteria. Food was different from what we were used to. We had a light fare and returned to our quarters. Our troop carrier hadn't yet been adapted to the comforts for civilian use. Our quarters consisted of a fairly large dormitory-style space with rows of double canvas bunks along the perimeter and in the middle of the room. The nearby bathroom included a row of showers with a central common area. I felt somewhat uncomfortable in the communal shower but I got used to it soon enough. The clean sheets were inviting as we slipped into them for a good night's sleep. I'm sure that we were all tired, if not physically, certainly emotionally.

I woke up few hours later feeling seasick. I ran to the bathroom and joined a few of the passengers who already had their heads over the sinks. Lightheaded and sick as dogs, we heaved out the contents of our stomachs. Ashen-faced, we slowly trickled back to our bunks, dropping wearily onto the thin mattresses. The next morning it seemed like a bad dream. Luckily this most unfortunate "group activity" didn't recur for the rest of the journey.

The afternoon sun revealed outlines of the next port city, Haifa, in the distance. British police monitored our ship as we approached the dock in Palestine. Disembarking passengers included a number of bearded men in the long black dress typical of Hasidic Jews. I presumed that they came from New York. Embarking passengers included a few people in similar garb. Luggage and chattel went both out of and into the ship.

The city of Haifa sat perched majestically on top of a small mountain. A winding paved road snaked from the harbor to the top of it. Just like Beirut there were homes and villas among green patches of citrus and olive trees. I stood against the deck railing in awe of the beauty before me, made even more glorious by the setting sun.

This is the land of milk and honey promised to our patriarch Abraham some 4,000 years before. This is where Moses brought the Israelites after being freed from the bondage of Pharaoh's Egypt. After 40 years of sojourn in the desert and dealing with the complaints of the twelve tribes, Moses was forbidden to enter.

44

He was instructed to climb a hill in the Jordan valley. God told him "You shall see it with your eyes, but there you shall not cross." I could not help hearing those words as the ship slowly bade goodbye to the cherished land of my ancestors. Tears were rolling down my face as we sailed away from the Promised Land.

The next day we approached Alexandria, Egypt in the afternoon. The ship docked for a few hours so we had time to leave if we wished. The port was full of hawkers aggressively selling everything including the kitchen sink from fruit and drinks to merchandise of all sorts. I had no difficulty understanding their language even though their dialect was decidedly different from the Arabic spoken in Baghdad. Eager to replace my cardboard suitcase more something more substantial, I haggled successfully for a handmade leather one that cost me approximately $10. The suitcase was the best thing I got out of Alexandria. What I saw of the city was a disappointment. It was a flat expanse interspersed with low buildings. Nothing stood out as memorable.

The ship slowly drifted into the deep blue of the Mediterranean in a northwesterly direction. It floated like a small toy boat in a large bathtub with a rhythmic up-and-down pitch of the bow. On a rare occasion we heard the horn blast of a ship passing by. We loved to wave to their passengers. It was both exciting and reassuring to know that we weren't alone in this watery microcosm.

Sunrise and sunset swept gracefully in and out - the arrival and departure of the Queen of the Heavens over an endless face of the deep. It was not difficult for me to fathom why so many people in ancient lands worshipped the sun.

My Journey on and off the Marine Carp

Upper left: The Parthenon. Upper right and lower left: waterfall and cave in Lebanon. Lower right: I am second from the left with my friends on July 23, 1947.

Our next stop was Piraeus, Greece. All of us yearned to set our feet firmly on dry land again. A small group of us young people banded together and hired a taxi. It was an old 1930s Ford with a canvas top. The driver packed as many of us as he could cram into his small vehicle. He drove us to the Parthenon and the other ancient Greek monuments on top of the Acropolis. The air was crystal clear and the sun shone brightly while we toured the area and took pictures. We were so exhilarated with the afternoon outing that one might think we sprung out of a dark jail.

Our next port and final destination, New York, was truly our "promised land." Exactly one month after I left Baghdad, I set foot on United States soil. Aside from my wedding day, August 8, 1947 is the most important day in my life, the day "the rest of my life" began.

Middlebury College, in front of the chemistry building, November 13, 1947

Part IV

1947-1949:
MIDDLEBURY COLLEGE

I left New York in mid-August, 1947 on a Greyhound bus to Middlebury, Vermont. The bus kept stopping in many small towns and hamlets, and I was afraid I'd miss my destination. I must have asked the driver one hundred times if Middlebury was the next stop. He kept telling me to be patient, and at last we arrived. I was dropped off on Route 7 near the center of town. I was a month too early for the start of school, so as of yet, I didn't have a place to stay. I spent the night in a home that had rooms for rent.

The next morning I walked about one mile east to the college and headed straight to the admissions office. They were very pleased to see me. The friendly admissions officer asked where I was staying until my dormitory room became available. He suggested I move closer to campus. His secretary, a newlywed living in a house nearby, offered me their extra room. The next day I moved. I carried my new leather suitcase from Egypt about half a mile to her house. My stay there was comfortable. I made an effort to stay out of their way and give them the privacy newlyweds deserve.

I couldn't have found a more convenient situation. There was a large grocery store in town where I purchased bread, milk, sardines, fruit, etc. For bed linen I went to the dry goods store in the town square. I struck up a conversation with the owner and his son and discovered that they were Jewish. I asked if there was a synagogue in town since the High Holidays of *Rosh Hashanah* and *Yom Kippur* were almost upon us. They told me that the town of Middlebury had only a few Jewish families and advised me to go 35 miles north to Burlington.

Just after school started, I went to the dean's office and asked to be excused for the Jewish High Holidays. I was right back on that Greyhound bus. I arrived in Burlington in the late afternoon. I walked up and down the streets trying to find out where the Jewish people lived. I kept asking passers-by, "Could you tell me how to get to the Jewish quarter?" Nobody seemed to understand what I was looking for! So I kept on walking and found myself in front of a butcher shop with Hebrew lettering in front, a very good indication that they sold kosher meat. I inquired as to where I could stay for the holidays. The owner asked me to wait for the rabbi, who would be coming in soon to pick up his order.

Enter Rabbi Whall. "Welcome to Burlington," said the gentleman, extending his hand to shake mine. "Jacob Shammash, from Baghdad, at Middlebury College," I offered in return. I'm quite sure he didn't meet people from Baghdad very often. He took me to his home, got on the phone to different members of his congregation, and found a family that would house me for the 2 days. I was very appreciative and thanked him.

The family was very hospitable. I had their son's bedroom to myself since he was away in the military. I joined them at synagogue the next morning, thankful to be in a Jewish place of worship on such an important day in the Hebrew calendar.

I enjoyed the services. They were going too fast for my knowledge of Hebrew, but I managed to keep up. They pronounced the Hebrew differently than what I was used to in Baghdad but the content of the service was similar. Their edifice was much smaller than our synagogue. The ark where the Torah scrolls were kept was adorned with brass on the sides. The seats were chairs whereas we had locally-made sofas in Baghdad covered with white sheets for the holidays and with Persian rugs in the winter.

My host family invited me to come back for *Yom Kippur*. I took them up on their kind offer. This time their son came home so I shared his room. I felt honored to sleep next to someone who had seen combat during a war that I only could imagine from reading the newspapers and listening to the radio. He didn't say very much about his experience. He was quite tired and no doubt thankful to be sleeping in his own bed in his own home.

I got up early the next morning, leaving him asleep. I thanked the family for their generosity. That evening I climbed back up onto the Greyhound bus. As we drove, I wished for peace in the world and a better future for those still suffering from the war. I looked forward to my studies at the college and hoped I'd do well.

Before school had started, I passed the days walking through the campus and soaking up my surroundings. It was all new to this Boy from Baghdad. The lush scenery was just beautiful. The Green Mountains, only a few miles away, lived up to their name. When the leaves started turning, I was dazzled by the bright red, yellow and orange colors.

Middlebury College

Top: In front of Munroe Hall, November 10, 1947. I am on the left. Bottom: In front of Mead Memorial Chapel. I am on the left. Right: The college wanted a picture of their foreign students. Here we are, playing in the snow. I'm on the right.

No sooner did those beautiful leaves fall from the trees, they were replaced by snowflakes. The sight was breathtaking. I never saw snow before in my life. I went from one extreme to the other, from the scorching heat to the coldest of colds. Soon more of the white stuff accumulated and remained for most of the long winter. Walking on the paths on cold bright days with sunlight reflecting off the snow and glinting on ice uplifted my soul. It gave me a small break from feeling bogged down with studies and looming end of semester exams.

I never stopped marveling at what nature had in store for me to enjoy, either as a bystander or a participant. Whenever I had time, I took long walks to immerse myself in the Vermont landscape, so foreign to my life experience until now.

I was assigned a room on the fourth floor of Star Hall, opposite the gymnasium. There was a corridor in the middle, a row of rooms on each side and a bathroom on each end. I had 2 roommates, both from the North Shore of Massachusetts. Our rooms were in the middle facing east. The bedroom had a bunk bed on one side and a single bed on the other. I ended up with the bottom of the bunk bed. The adjacent room, reserved for studying, held our 3 desks.

Each morning I would arise earlier than my roommates, head for the study room and lock the door behind me. Then I donned my *tallit* and *tefillin* to say my morning prayers. Afterwards, I woke my roommates to go for breakfast.

One morning, while I was praying in the study room with the door locked, my roommates happened to get up on their own. They were on their way to breakfast. They needed some books, so they banged on the door. I quickly removed the *tallit* and *tefillin* and put them away prior to opening the door. All the while they continued to bang, "Open up already! We're late for breakfast!" I didn't want them to see me in my prayer outfit, figuring that they probably didn't know anything about Jewish traditions.

We set out together for breakfast. The dining hall was on the hill to the right of the chapel. It opened at 7am and the doors were promptly closed 10 minutes later. No latecomers were permitted. On the occasional morning when we ran late, my 2 roommates, large, muscular and more able-bodied than me, raced down the 4 flights like the wind. They conquered the hill so fast that when I tried to catch up, I became winded. By the time I sat down for breakfast I felt weak and ready to pass out. I hurried to the bathroom, quickly lay down on the ground and sure enough, I briefly lost consciousness. Breakfast wasn't worth the agony! After all, I was about 5'5" and weighed no more than 115 lbs.

My roommates and I had different patterns. I typically did my homework after supper and finished by about 10pm. They didn't settle down to study until late, by which time I was almost done. By the second semester I decided to get my own room. I was lucky to get one just across the hall. It would be easier for me to study as well as to keep my kosher diet.

Instead of going to the dining room, where I only ate dairy products anyway, I could go to the grocery store in town and get milk, butter, eggs, sardine cans, fruit, and whatever else I needed. I purchased a hot plate and made 2 soft-boiled eggs every morning. I boiled the water in a glass beaker that I got from the chemistry lab. I kept the milk and butter on the sill outside the window, which served as my private refrigerator.

I took my studies very seriously. Writing and math classes were mandatory. The entire freshman class had to take entrance exams for placement in the class of their aptitude level. I started at the entry level in English because my results weren't great. I performed better on the math exam so I started a notch above. I enjoyed all of my courses. I loved chemistry and breezed through the first year. Physics was tougher. I didn't take any history. Since I didn't learn French in Baghdad I began it here and took it all through my years at Middlebury.

I earned enough credits to graduate in only 2 years, bridged with the summer session of 1948.

I don't mean to make it sound like all I did at Middlebury was work, pray and stick to myself. That wasn't the case at all! I wasn't social, but I had plenty of friends. The other students were very accepting of me. I enjoyed football games with friends on weekends. On winter nights after finishing homework, a lot of the students went downstairs and skated under flood lights. Star Hall had an ice skating rink right in front. I watched them from my fourth floor window with curiosity followed by envy. I bought skates and joined in, slowly teaching myself how to glide on the ice.

Winter Carnival was by far the most exciting event. Middlebury had a ski slope not far from the college. They boasted the highest ski jump in the area. Ice sculptures, snow shoes, skates and skis were all new words in my vocabulary.

Although I didn't ski in college, I learned with my children when they were young. We were lucky enough to live very close to Mt. Tom in Holyoke, only 17 minutes from our house. We enjoyed that little mountain for many years. Sadly, it closed a while ago. It was also a great pleasure for me to take them to Middlebury's Winter Carnivals where I could relive my good times through their eyes.

My short time at Middlebury College was among the best years of my life. Needless to say, I was pleased that my daughter Ellen chose my Alma Mater. Her middle daughter, Amanda, graduated from Middlebury in June of 2017. I hope the legacy continues.

Part V

1947-1950S:
PARTITION OF PALESTINE AND
TOUGH TIMES FOR IRAQI JEWS

While I was preparing to come to the U.S., the United Nations pondered the fate of Palestine. The British prepared to relinquish their mandate, in effect since WWI, after having liberated most of the Middle East from the rule of the Ottoman Empire. The Zionists were settling refugees from eastern and central Europe throughout most of Palestine from the Galilee to the Negev. They were instrumental in pushing the British out of the area by inciting multiple uprisings against them. The Arabs, on the other hand, were clashing against the Jewish immigrants to discourage their settlement. They were intent on keeping all of Palestine to themselves.

The Security Council of the U.N. eventually voted on the Partition Plan which gave the Jewish people the western portion, and the Arabs, the eastern portion of Palestine. The Jews accepted the plan. The Arabs rejected it, calling on their people to abandon their homes and go eastward to Jordan and east of the Jordan River. Through the Arab League, they rallied the Arab states of the region to fight against the newly formed Jewish state.

On May 14, 1948, the state of Israel declared itself an independent Jewish state with Ben Gurion as President. President Truman immediately gave his support, making the United States the first major country of the U.N. to acknowledge the Jewish state. One day later, on May 15th, the neighboring Arab states marshalled their armies and invaded Israel. The fledging Israel Defense Forces, comprised of members of the *Haganah* and *Irgun* resistance groups, fended off the invading Arab armies.

The Iraqi units returned home, dejected. Once Israel was established, they looked upon their own Jews as enemies in their midst who would become Zionists and therefore traitors. Never mind that the Jewish community in Baghdad had been established for more than 2,600 years and that Iraqi Jews felt just as "Iraqi" as anyone else. The government took out their wrath on their own (Jewish) citizens, especially in the big cities of Baghdad, Mosul and Basra. Even before the U.N. declared the Partition Plan, anti-Semitism escalated in Baghdad in the summer and fall of 1947. It came to a head in 1948 and 1949. Many Iraqi Jews, especially the young, saw no future in their homeland. Many planned to leave the country but as time went on, the government made it harder and harder for them to go.

While I was in Middlebury, many of the Jews in Baghdad began selling their homes in preparation to leave. My grandfather, uncles, and to a lesser extent, my father, began shifting money out of the country. They had to transfer funds abroad through trusted Arabs for a fee of one third of the total amount. My relatives began sending me as much as they could. Overnight I became their personal banker. I deposited their money in a savings bank in the town of Middlebury, diligently keeping a record of each account in a tiny notebook with a black cover. I remember this just as if it happened yesterday. As soon as I received a check, I walked a mile or so to the little town bank. It was my good deed to all of my family members in time of their need. It gave me a sense of accomplishment and a tremendous uplift of the soul to know that even "little me" could be of help even though I was about 8,000 miles away.

Toward the end of 1948, my father started to lose vision in one of his eyes. The local eye doctors couldn't help him. He elected to travel to London for treatment. It took him a few months to get a passport. He found out that he had a retinal detachment. The operation on his eye entailed both mobilization of the orbit and relieving the coagulated fluid in the back of the retina with a cautery needle inserted through the back of the eye. After surgery he remained in bed with sandbags on each side of his head to keep it motionless for a full month.

Not long after he left the hospital in London, his eyesight in the treated eye got so bad that he was reduced to seeing only shadows. For the next few months he lived near Liverpool with old friends from Baghdad who left before WWII. He was very happy to re-establish his friendship.

Jan. '49
Rhyl, Flintshire
ENGLAND

My father spent time with friends in Rhyl, Flintshire, in England after having eye surgery.

Rationing in England continued long after the war and made life very difficult for its inhabitants. My father asked me to send as much as I could, items including rice, tea and coffee. I would go to the general store, buy several one pound cartons of rice (for example), carry them back to the dormitory, properly package them in brown paper made from cut-up shopping bags and tie the bundle with strong cord. I shipped multiple such packages at his request for more supplies increased. My father must have given these packages to many of his friends.

Before too long my father started to lose vision in his "good" eye. The doctors told him it was retinal detachment all over again. He had always been dear to me, which made me all the more sad that he could barely see anything. He was put through the same operative routine and prolonged convalescence to no advantage, but he remained hopeful. Upon continued investigation, he learned that there was a certain doctor in Utrecht in the Netherlands who was the expert in his condition. He went there for surgery but again it was to no avail. His world plunged from seeing only shadows to total darkness.

He went back to London and Liverpool where socializing with his old cronies boosted his morale. I was pleased to receive cheerful mail from him. Time marched on. During his 2 year absence my oldest brother assumed the role of temporary surrogate dad for the rest of the family. My mother was home with her younger children awaiting the return of her now blind husband.

The news from Baghdad was not encouraging. Not so slowly, but very surely, Iraqi Jews were stripped of their rights: assets frozen, expelled from municipal and government jobs, restricted as to their own private businesses, unable to attend schools of higher education, unable to sell their homes, unable to travel freely, and above all, unable to leave the country. Many Jews worked in banks and transportation, especially the railway system that had been built by the British and spanned the country from the northern city of Mosul to the southern port city of Basra. They were all fired. A considerable number were reduced from middle income to poverty levels.

In March of 1950, then Prime Minister Nuri al-Said issued the Denaturalization Act. Before this, Jews weren't allowed to leave the country. He offered them an "opportunity." They could leave and in the process, forfeit their Iraqi citizenship and all their assets. The authorities were expecting no more than 10,000 people to take advantage of this draconian decree. They were flabbergasted when 40,000 applicants applied in the first month. Now they had to deal with an overwhelming number of "new aliens," too many to process in the 2 week period they had set for them to leave. For administrative purposes they had no choice but to extend the 2 weeks to one year. Those who waited to leave were interned in refugee camps.

Most of the refugees went to Israel. Others who could afford the passage money and had family or friends abroad joined them in London, Paris, the United States or in Canada. Having been apprised of the deteriorating situation, many students already abroad chose to stay in their respective new environments. Other young people with a Zionist zeal left home in darkness, made their way either across the western desert or eastward to Iran, and eventually to Palestine where they joined the ranks of the *Kibbutzim* (collective communities, usually agricultural) or the *Haganah* (a Jewish paramilitary organization in the British Mandate of Palestine [1921–48], which became the core of the IDF, the Israel Defense Forces).

Although, and in spite of being overwhelmed by a swelling tide of refugees, the Israeli government launched an airlift in March of 1951. It was called "Operation Nehemiah and Azaria," named for 2 of the prophets of Judah who brought consolation to the Israelites as they were driven out of their homeland and marched as captives into Babylonia 2,600 years ago. Two airplanes were made available daily. One left Baghdad for Lod Airport in Israel. The other headed back to Baghdad.

Between 1948 and 1951 approximately 121,633 Jews left Iraq. 60,000 of those left after the Prime Minister's decree. Only 15,000 Jews remained in the entire country. Ultimatums took the form of an elastic band, contracting and expanding at the whim of a dictatorial government. The law expired in March of 1951 but was later extended. In 1952 emigration to Israel was again banned. The Iraqi government publicly hanged 2 Jews who had been falsely charged with throwing a bomb at the Baghdad office of the U.S. Information Agency.

My father eventually left England and returned home. At the time of the Denaturalization Act, he had very little cash. His vast holdings were tied up in real estate, the value of which had increased significantly in the post-war years. The decision to stay or leave Baghdad was a real dilemma for him. At stake was all his property and his lifelong accomplishments. If he were to leave Iraq he could only take a suitcase with a few necessities and a very limited amount of cash equivalent to about $5 per person. After a few months he told himself that things were quieting down. Even though most of the Jews had left, he had a nucleus of friends to meet at the local coffee shops. He felt secure in the warmth of his own home with his family.

My maternal grandfather decided early on to leave to Israel with the majority of his friends and neighbors. He settled in Holon, a town not too far from Tel-Aviv. Except for my mother, his firstborn who remained in Baghdad, all his children and grandchildren were nestled around him. Some of them sold their homes at a ridiculously low value because of the glut on the market, given that most Jewish families were doing the same. Those who couldn't sell left their homes in my brother's care so he could do his best to sell them.

One by one my brothers and sisters started to leave home. Samra left for England in October of 1951. She got her degree with honors in organic chemistry from Southampton University (part of the University of London). Several years later Rachele set forth to Southampton University where she obtained a chemistry degree. My oldest brother told Maurice to go to Israel and promised that he and the younger children would follow.

I think back only 3 years to my departure from Baghdad. I had all my family around me as I boarded a first class air conditioned bus. The refitted war ship may not have been luxury but it did the trick. My 2 week journey was all about making friends and having fun sightseeing. Maurice's experience only a few years later was entirely different from mine. He was barely 18 years old when he left Baghdad for Israel in June of 1951. Little did he know of the hardship and anguish that awaited him.

Before I recount Maurice's story I must mention that not all of my siblings were forthcoming with theirs. Some were kind to grant me permission to use photographs in which they appear, but they prefer to keep their experiences private. I am respectful of their wishes.

Maurice was ready to head for college before the decree of 1950, a time when Jews trying to leave were under great suspicion. The timing couldn't have been worse. In 1949, he was taken from his home, put under arrest, and held for 9 day. It took a full year before he was brought before a tribunal. Thirteen Jews were in the same situation as he was. Each of them had their own lawyer. All of them were cleared of trumped-up charges.

By now, Jews could go to Israel. In June of 1951, Maurice and two cousins headed to the airport to leave Baghdad for Israel. When they arrived they saw large groups formed outside (there was no terminal). The cousins were directed to one group, and Maurice, to another. He didn't see them again for the rest of the trip.

It was morning and the summer heat was already unbearable.

Everyone baked in the sun, but for Maurice it was almost deadly. Only allowed one suitcase, he had worn virtually all the clothing he owned. Only his face was discernable under 15 (no exaggeration) layers of shirts, vests, sweaters and suits. A plane, leaking oil, flew in and out with a group of passengers. Maurice was left waiting for another plane, and by the looks of the one that had already come, he worried seriously about whether these dubious-looking vehicles could complete the journey in one piece.

Scared to death, he continued baking in the blazing sun all day and through the evening. At about 10pm, his plane arrived. Fifty or 60 passengers boarded the small plane to find that there were no seats. They were packed in like sheep in the confined, airless space. It was so claustrophobic that Maurice tried desperately to break one of the windows for air.

Several hours later they arrived in Israel. Maurice kneeled down and kissed the ground.

The newcomers were led into a huge tent where they were sprayed with some kind of disinfectant chemical. Maurice, who left his stately home, felt as welcome as a vagabond. After being sprayed the whole group was moved to another tent for the night. They found a sea of small stretchers (with only 6 inches between each of them) on which to sleep.

Morning came. The bewildered refugees were told to locate their suitcases. Maurice found his – opened. Apparently it was so full that it sprung open when it was plunked down. Not only was he surprised to find it open; the contents baffled him even more. Back in Baghdad some officials helped themselves to all of his documents, papers, and whatever else held interest for them, and replaced those items with pots and pans!

After a pitiful breakfast, people were told to board one of the many trucks waiting outside. Maurice asked the driver where they were being taken. His response was a shrug of the shoulders. Maurice refused to get on the truck. He waited around for hours. At 3:30pm the last truck pulled in. He was told that he could either get on that truck or suffer another night on one of the stretchers in the tent. Maurice got on the truck.

The mystery ride took the passengers to Haifa. The greeting there was just as inhospitable as it had been 2 days before at the airport. They were herded into a large area circled with barbed wire, a sort of "camp" policed by officials. All of the suitcases were unloaded in a pile.

Maurice was frantic. He tried to tell one of the officials that he needed to find his cousins. His suitcase was too heavy for him to lift, so he said he'd leave it there while he went off to look for them. A woman nearby overheard the conversation. She motioned to Maurice. "Look," she told him. "If you leave that suitcase, you'll never see it again. Have someone bring it close to my tent ("her" tent had about a dozen people in it) and I'll watch it for you.

He had no recourse but to trust her. He used the two packs of cigarettes and equivalent of $20, all that he was allowed to take out of Baghdad, as *baksheesh* to get one of the guards to move his suitcase. He went off to look for his cousins but he couldn't find them. He learned that they were taken to a camp south of Tel Aviv.

Despondent, he went back to the woman's tent. "Tent" was a kind word for this tarp stretched on poles with no sides. He stayed with her and the others. After a while, she confided in him. "I can't stand this place either. Here's what I've done. During the nights I began digging a tunnel under the barbed wire so once it was finished, I could sneak out. You can use it too!"

Maurice was dying to get out of there. Once on the other side, he could jump on a bus go to the beach or simply enjoy the city of Haifa. He hadn't had a good meal since he left Baghdad. Strictly kosher, he had never eaten outside his own home or that of a family member. He wondered what it would be like to go to a restaurant. This is Israel, he thought to himself. I'm sure the food is kosher. Imagine his surprise and horror when he picked up a menu and saw that pork and ham were served! He lost his appetite.

Maurice still remembers this as the worst time to have been in Israel. The fledging state was flooded with refugees and very few resources. There wasn't much food so there was rationing. Everyone got coupons. Each person was entitled to one egg and one ounce of meat per week. There were long lines for staples including bread.

When Maurice located his cousins from Mosul, the 3 of them decided to live together. Things were tough, but he was determined to put his time to good use. In order to improve his Hebrew he took night courses at the Technion-Israel Institute of Technology in Haifa. Established during the Ottoman Empire in 1912, it is the oldest university in Israel.

Maurice was more than ready to leave Israel. He had been miserably lonely and homesick since he left Baghdad. Although our oldest brother promised to come with everyone, our parents wouldn't leave, so he stayed behind to take care of them. Maurice contacted a lawyer to see what he'd have to do to go to the U.S. The answer was grim. He would need about $5,000.

Maurice mulled over his situation. He left Baghdad with no papers of identity. He was stateless. He knew, however, that if he joined one of the Israeli forces and served the required 2-1/2 years that he would be given an Israeli passport. With that, he could go wherever he wanted. He joined the Air Force. He was clever, industrious, and a great mechanic. He continued taking night classes and worked in the engineering department where he learned to repair old British jets from WWII, called Meteor.

When he finished his time with the Air Force he was ready to go to the United States. He had received an acceptance at MIT in Cambridge, Massachusetts. He went to the U.S. Consulate in Haifa to apply for a visa. He was kept waiting for over four months. Finally he went back again and was told that he was refused. The head of the embassy conducted a thorough check on his family and found out that he already had a brother in the States (me) who came as a student but never left. That simply couldn't happen again.

Denied his U.S. visa, Maurice went to the British Embassy, obtained a visa, and spent 4 years attending London University.

Some time passed. Samra was getting married in Boston on July 17, 1959. He hadn't seen her for 8-1/2 years and he desperately wanted to go to the wedding.

He went to the U.S. Embassy in London. After his experience in Haifa he knew enough to wait until he could spot someone who looked sympathetic. He approached a woman who told him that he could have a four week visa to go to the U.S. under several conditions. He had to buy a return ticket to London and have a job and/or enough money to live there upon his return. He did

Maurice in the Israeli Air Force

March 5, 1953

Back in Baghdad

Top: Joyce and Shaul, March 25, 1954. Bottom: Their wedding in June of 1955. David and Jeanette are seated in front.

Habbaniyah

An excursion to Habbaniyah, April, 1955. Our car is a Nash. From left to right: Joyce, Shaul, Sami, David, Eliahou and Jeanette

Out of Baghdad

Samra in Hastings, England, 1952. Maurice in Haifa, October 15, 1954

what he was told and prepared for his trip. It was only a few days before the wedding.

Shortly after his plane took off, one propeller went up in flames. It was even less encouraging when the second propeller caught fire as well. The plane turned around and landed in Ireland.

He made the wedding by the skin of his teeth. Then he thumbed his nose at that miserable U.S. Embassy official back in Haifa. He intended to make the U.S. his home.

It was 1959 and I now had 2 siblings in Boston. Maurice had arrived. Samra was working on her graduate degree in chemistry at Radcliffe College in Cambridge. Our mother missed us terribly and wanted to come visit. I hadn't seen her for 9 years. She was able to get a passport and visa, so all of us were in luck.

She did not say too much about the situation back home and nothing about the mass emigration in 1950 of 95 percent of the Iraqi Jewish population. Aliza had been through so much. Only 48 years old, her family was scattered. Of her 9 children, about half were in the United States. She was very close to her own family, now all in Israel. When they lived near us in the eastern part of Baghdad we visited them every Saturday afternoon. Those days were forever gone. She constantly worried about her blind husband and the future of her family.

She stayed just a few weeks. Although she was thrilled to see us, she grew eager to return home to care for her husband. She went back hoping that there would be a day when her family would be reunited.

On July 14, 1958 elements of the army raided the king's palace early one morning, seized the young King Faisal II and his uncle, the regent Abd al-Ilah and massacred both of them on the lawn of the palace.

The next few years were calm. The new ruler grew up among Jews and respected them. An attempt to assassinate him in 1963 was foiled. The perpetrators were members of the Ba'ath party, none other than young Saddam Hussein and his Uncle Ahmad Hassan al-Bakr. Both flew out of the country seeking asylum in Syria, a Ba'ath stronghold.

They came back and staged a successful coup in 1968. Ahmed Hassan al-Bakr became the new president of Iraq with all the ideology of the Ba'ath party, complete with hatred of Jews and Israel. A military court tried 14 men, 9 of them Jewish. All were executed in a public square in Baghdad. Just off to the side, President Al-Bakr led a crowd of a quarter million in song and dance as they watched the "Zionist spies" hanged.

Frightened, the Jews remained locked up in their homes. After this episode they wanted *out*. It was common to wake up in the morning and find out that imperceptibly and without a trace, neighbors had fled during the night. The end of the first Kurdish-Iraqi war in 1970 opened a new escape route. For enough *baksheesh* given to top officials in the Iranian government, Iranian borders were open to escaping Jewish refugees.

Part VI

1949-1970s:
MY LIFE UNFOLDS

I attended the University of Buffalo School of Medicine (now part of the State University of New York system, it's known as SUNY Buffalo) from September, 1949 through June, 1953. After graduation I chose to stay at a hospital in Buffalo for another year to do my required rotating internship before residency. Every few months we learned different specialties: medicine, surgery, pediatrics, OBGYN, orthopedics, neurology and psychiatry.

Surgery was my calling. I applied to the Beth Israel Hospital in Boston (now the Beth Israel Deaconess Medical Center, formed out of the 1996 merger of the Beth Israel and the New England Deaconess). It was and still is the teaching hospital of Harvard Medical School. I was accepted by Dr. Jacob Fine, chief of surgery and worked there from 1954 to 1957. My rotation of surgical service included independent surgical procedures in the operating room, at times under the guidance of members of the visiting staff of Harvard and Tufts medical schools.

Buffalo Medical School

1949

Buffalo Children's Hospital
April, 1952

Having fun with my colleagues. I am on the left.

We were married in Estelle's home in Bangor, Maine on March 18, 1955.

During this time, I had an interesting encounter with a young lady in the food line at the hospital cafeteria. A lab technician, she was dressed in her white uniform. I heard her complain to the attendant behind the food counter that the hardboiled egg she held was "rotten," brown and discolored. She couldn't be expected to eat *that*.

She had a pretty face with pink cheeks. I was attracted not only by her good looks but by her firm argumentative assertion. *Carpe diem!* I jumped at this fortuitous opportunity. I expressed my deepest sympathy to her. Indeed, the egg was overcooked, somewhat toasted. I wasn't a picky eater. I offered to take the egg so she could choose something more palatable. Problem solved, the young lass followed her friends and sat down for lunch. Normally shy and unassuming, I followed her and sat down to properly introduce myself. Extending a hand, I told her my name was Jacob. Hers was Estelle. "See," I told her as I peeled the shell from the egg, "there's nothing wrong with it. It just got toasted and turned from white to brown. By the way, this is my weekend off. I'm going for a ride to the North Shore. Would you join me?"

Estelle recounted the story to her oldest daughter many years later. She was intrigued, but there was no way that she would take off for the day with a man she didn't know. She turned it into a double-date. She obviously had a good time, because she told my daughter that a month after we met, she knew she was going to marry me. I was (happily) caught hook, line and sinker long before I knew it!

We were married in her home in Bangor, Maine on March

18, 1955. Her mother, Sarah, liked me well enough, though when we got engaged I learned that she asked Estelle, "Can't you find an American boy?!" She adored her daughter, whom she called "Queen Esther." Sarah came to Boston to visit us when our first child was 2 years old. She never left. "Nana" was a gem, helping her daughter raise our 5 children. She was part of our household until shortly before she died at the age of 88. All of us were bereft.

The day of the wedding there was a huge blizzard raging through New England. I had to drive from Boston to Bangor, more than 7 hours' drive on a good day given the road in those days. I was told that poor Estelle kept peering out of the windows wondering if I would make it. I did, and as it turns out, we usually celebrated our anniversaries with a big blizzard until we moved to Florida for the winter.

In the late 1950s hospitals paid their resident house staff very little. I earned $12 a week and Estelle made a whopping $60 as a lab technician. We rented a tiny basement apartment, a makeshift lodging with very sparse furnishings, in the home of the Commandant of the Chelsea Soldiers Home. Our only source of heat in the winter was the gas stove in the kitchen. The commandant's wife, Jean, befriended Estelle and often invited her upstairs to chat over coffee. The Quigley's were very good to us.

At the Beth Israel there was a pyramidal system to get the job of chief resident. One had to fulfill this position to become a member of the Society of General Surgery. I would have to wait my turn and waste a year of my time doing lab work. I wasn't interested. I knew I had to perform the required 2 years of service with the army or navy so I decided to get that over with during this juncture.

I was stationed at the Portsmouth, New Hampshire Naval Hospital which was actually located in Kittery, Maine. I worked with the chief of surgery doing small procedures such as hernias and appendectomies. The big surgery was performed at the Naval Hospital in Boston. I was in Portsmouth in September of 1957 when Estelle went into labor. It was Jean Quigley who took Estelle to the Beth Israel to deliver our first child.

When I left the Navy in 1959 it was time to take the position of chief resident. One could do this in a particular specialty, which for me, was surgery. After I performed 2 years of chest surgery at the Boston City Hospital, finishing in June of 1961, I went back to the Beth Israel as an "attending thoracic surgeon." All training finished, it was time for me to find "my real job."

Surgeons need referrals, and as the new kid on the block, I found getting them to be really difficult. Everyone else was already established and had their networks. Plus, doctors were a dime a dozen in Boston. I was a tiny fish in the big ocean. Someone suggested that I go to Springfield to set up shop. They weren't glutted with doctors in Western Massachusetts and no one was doing pacemakers there. I had a chance to be a bigger fish in a smaller bowl.

Estelle and I decided it was worth heading west on the Mass Pike to check this place out. Neither of us was enthralled. She had all her friends in Boston and there was nothing there for her. She knew full well that a surgeon's wife, especially one of my

I was stationed at the Portsmouth Naval Hospital in Kittery, Maine.

Our first child, Amy, was born on September 20, 1957 while I was still in the Navy.

specialty, would spend most of her time alone. We headed back east to the Boston we loved. A year later, however, we realized that like it or not, we needed to make a change. We moved to Springfield in 1962.

It wasn't easy settling into work in the Springfield hospitals. I worked in the Mercy Hospital emergency room for 3 years to supplement the income from my new practice. Over time both my practice and my family continued to grow. We welcomed our fifth and last child, Elizabeth, on May 3, 1970. We had 4 daughters and a son.

In the early years I worked at several hospitals: Springfield Hospital (now Baystate Medical Center), the Noble (now Baystate Noble, Westfield), Holyoke Hospital and Cooley-Dickinson (Northampton). I lived out of my car. I always kept a razor in the glove compartment to shave here and there, especially if sundown approached on a Friday and I was still out on the town. One isn't allowed to shave on the *Shabbat*.

On the infrequent evenings I made it home for dinner, I was inevitably called out with an emergency. It could have been the gunshot wounds that were common after pay day, a collapsed lung or complications of some sort. In my line of work, whatever it was, it was always an emergency. Exasperated, Estelle would say, "Can't you finish your dinner first?"

In spite of my lengthy hours and erratic schedule, Estelle was the great promoter of my career. Very social, she was quick to make friends and soon surrounded herself with other doctor's wives. In the mid to late 1960s she threw elaborate cocktail parties for my colleagues and their wives. This was the time of Audrey

Hepburn and "Breakfast at Tiffany's." Elegance and style were top priority. Women came dressed to the nines in gowns and furs.

We were obliged to put out ashtrays in those days because people still smoked. My own wife was famous for "bumming" cigarettes from friends when I was nowhere in sight. She reasoned that the wife of a lung surgeon couldn't possibly buy a pack of her own but taking a cigarette from someone else "didn't count." She quit as soon as the general public became aware of smoking hazards.

We had a laundry room downstairs which had a window cut out to the den. Helpers set up the bar there and would pass drinks through that window to the guests. People drank hard liquor with the hors d'oeuvres that flowed in a steady stream from the kitchen, served on silver trays by waitresses dressed in uniform.

Our kids just loved those parties. Estelle dressed them up and turned them into "coat girls." When guests arrived, they took the women's' fur coats, usually mink or seal, and put them on top of their brother's bed upstairs. I daresay they tried on a few, like playing dress-up, before putting them down. They didn't want to miss a trick so when they got tired they changed into their pajamas and brought their blankets and pillows to the top of the staircase where they could watch the goings-on.

I performed pacemaker implants throughout my 38 year career in Springfield. I was chief of thoracic surgery at the (then) Springfield Hospital from 1964-1976. I implanted well over 1,000 of them. I had the heyday for pacemakers, for later in my career they were implanted by invasive cardiologists. The surgeon no longer performed this task. Back then the device was a real clunker, a circular shape about 3 inches wide and a good inch thick. For my 80th birthday I was surprised with a very special one indeed. We have a dear friend, Pat Cohen, who is more creative, clever and energetic than anyone else I know. Estelle gave her an old pacemaker that was probably stuck in a drawer somewhere. Pat used it as the centerpiece of a "sailor's valentine," an intricate craft using sea shells to create something beautiful and intensely personal to be given with love. It is one of the most beautiful gifts I have ever received.

My work became inextricably linked with who I am, so I feel that it should be included in my memoir. I will offer detailed information followed by a simplification. If the reader isn't interested, feel free to skip the rest of this chapter.

The Pacemaker

Before pacemakers were implanted they were worn externally. In April of 1960, implanted or indwelling pacemakers were approved in America for use in humans. In 1962, while I was still at the Beth Israel Hospital, I had the distinction of assisting Dr. Howard Frank, Assistant Chief of Surgery and a thoracic surgeon, in the implantation of the very first pacemaker in the hospital. This pacemaker was developed by Dr. Paul Zoll, a cardiologist at the hospital.

Born in Boston in 1911 to devout Jewish parents who had emigrated from Lithuania and Belarus, Dr. Zoll attended Harvard for undergraduate training in psychology and then the Harvard Medical School. He practiced at the Beth Israel for his entire career where he pioneered the technique of applying electric shocks to the surface of the chest when the heart needed stimulation.

Collaborating with Alan Belgard, electrical engineer and co-owner of the Electrodyne Company, he developed the artificial cardiac pacemaker and cardiac defibrillator. Dr. Zoll, who passed away in 1999, was felt to be the father of modern electrocardiac therapy.[5]

I was in the right place at the right time to have trained with such a brilliant heart specialist.

The first indwelling pacemaker units consisted of a battery powered pacemaker with 2 wires connected to it. The wires had needles at the end. They were insulated, all except for a 2 cm area that was *not* insulated. Each needle was sutured to the muscle of that left ventricle (chamber) and pulled enough to allow the uninsulated portion of the wire to remain within the left ventricle muscle. Their position was secured by silk sutures on each end and the needles were clipped off. The pericardium (double-walled sac containing the heart and the roots of the great vessels) was closed. Then the rib cage was closed. Surgery took 1-1/2 to 2 hours.

In simpler terms, we used traditional surgery to implant these devices. First, we put the patient to sleep with anesthesia. Next, we opened up the patient's rib cage so that we could see inside the patient's body and open up the pericardium (sac around the heart). While the heart was beating, we would then attach the two electric wires directly to the patient's heart muscle. Then we would sew up the pericardium and the rib cage, letting the pacemaker wires

---

[5] https://en.wikipedia.org/wiki/Paul_Zoll

pass to the outside of this area where they would attach to the pacemaker. The pacemaker would sit underneath the patient's skin but outside of the rib cage. It looked like a large bump underneath the skin of the upper chest. The battery powered pacemaker could then send gentle shock waves through these wires to help the heart beat on a regular basis.

These pacemakers weren't very good. They took a mercury-zinc battery which only lasted a year or two. The casing, made of epoxy, wasn't a tight seal. When someone needed a new pacemaker, an incision would be made under the skin. The old pacemaker would be replaced with a new one. The wires were not replaced – unless they broke. The Cordis pacemaker (Cordis was founded in Miami) would be improved upon, but throughout my career I preferred the wires they made.

When I relocated to Springfield, I implanted the first pacemaker there in 1964. Unfortunately, the Mercy Hospital didn't keep this new gizmo in stock. I had to order the pacemaker equipment directly from the Cordis supply company in Boston. They put the device on the Peter Pan Bus to send it to Springfield. When the bus arrived I had to drive to the station and pick it up! (Peter Picknelly was the founder of the Peter Pan Bus Company. I operated on him and we became good friends). The unit was clean but not sterile. We immersed it in alcohol overnight. The next day it was ready for use.

Some 10 years later technology improved along with the implanting procedure. A better product became available when Cardia Pacemakers, Inc. (CPI, now Guidant) of Minneapolis designed the world's first lithium-iodide cell powered pacemaker in 1972. I implanted the first such unit that year. They lasted 10 to

20 years in my patients. The new device also had a hermetically sealed case made from titanium.

Medtronic Corporation in Minneapolis improved the units and the lithium power supply and emerged as king of pacemakers and later on of cardioverters. In the late 1970s, I switched entirely to using Medtronic products. (Today, Medtronic Corporation, also in Minneapolis, produces most of the world's lithium batteries used in pacemakers and defibrillators. The Cordis Corporation (Guidant) continues to make all kinds of excellent leads (wires).

In the 1970s, we also began to use a new pacemaker insertion procedure. Two wires were used, one in the right auricle (also called the atrium) and one in the right ventricle. Each of the pacemaker's 2 wires was inserted using a needle thrusted under the clavicle (collar bone) into the axillary vein and then threaded into the superior vena cava, the vein that drains blood from the arms and head. One wire was fed through the superior vena cava into the right auricle then through the tricuspid valve into the right ventricle to be anchored near the apex or tip of the ventricle. An external pacing unit was connected to the wire. Using small electrical signals, we moved the position of this wire until the optimal position was found to pace the heart with the lowest amount of electrical current. The second wire was positioned in the right auricle using a similar method. The positions of both wires were then secured by sutures around them near the clavicle. The pacemaker was attached to the 2 wires and stored in a pocket under the skin. The pacemaker was able to send separate electrical signals through each wire, first to the auricle and then to the ventricle with a few millisecond delay, helping the right auricle to contract just moments before the right ventricle, just like in a normal heart.

In summary, this new pacemaker implantation system developed in the 1970s was better than the original 1960s technique because we could get the pacemaker wires into the heart more easily. Inserting the wires through a needle into the veins of the upper chest did *not* require general anesthesia. We did *not* have to open up the rib cage or the pericardium. This was a safer, quicker, and gentler procedure which was much easier for me and my patients.

As I mentioned earlier, pacemakers are now implanted by invasive cardiologists in a much simpler procedure. In 1972 the units were large, about 6x12x1.5 cm, hermetically sealed inside a shiny metal case. Nowadays the units are very small, a little larger than a 25 cent coin. The leads (wires) were also improved; breakage was reduced to almost zero.

Part VII

THE 1970s:
THE REST OF MY FAMILY
ARRIVES FROM BAGHDAD

While my career and my family bloomed, those left in Baghdad were scared for their lives. Along with my parents, my 2 elder brothers remained with their wives and children.

My parents came to Boston in 1962 and intended to stay. In 1964, however, the Iraqi government informed them that their travel visas wouldn't be renewed. If they didn't go back to Iraq they would relinquish their citizenship and their assets. They felt that they had too much at stake. They headed home.

In 1966 I became a U.S. citizen and with that new status, I would be able to get visas for my family to come back. They were welcome as long as I took financial responsibility for them. I begged them, but my father wanted to stay home. Hindsight is 20/20. They knew things were bad but they kept hopes that the terrible times would blow over. My father still had some buddies to socialize with. And so they stayed.

My Eldest Nephew

I am recounting my nephew's story from his own words. At his request, he and his family members are not named.

My nephew was 16 in 1972 and in his last year of high school. Out of the 50 or 60 students, only 17 remained, the majority having left over the previous 3 years. He rode his bicycle home from school one day in October, arriving at about 2pm. He saw a man waiting outside the front door. His mother was distraught. "They've come to take your father 'for questioning'." Both of them knew what that meant. Since Rosh Hashanah, barely a month ago, 20 people had been taken.

He remembers watching his father collect some basic belongings. He and his mother stood still, stunned and horrified, as my oldest brother walked out of the door. The man accompanied him to a small car waiting down the street, one of the vehicles belonging to the Secret Service. The driver got out of the car to usher his father into the back seat. They drove him away, never to be seen or heard from again. Two attempts made by his mother to look for him failed. The second time they threatened to arrest her if she tried to find him again. To this day, I can't bear to think about what happened to my kind, loving brother.

As soon as I received this horrible news I started looking for help. I wrote to the U.S. Ambassador to the United Nations, a man named George Herbert Walker Bush. He was quite sympathetic, understanding my pain and urgency. He replied with a nice letter but since the U.S. didn't have representation in Iraq, he was powerless to help.

Meanwhile, my nephew finally got his passport and left in May, 1973. He was ticketed from Baghdad to Beirut because he didn't need a visa to travel to Lebanon. However, the airport in Beirut had been bombed the previous night so the plane was diverted to Cyprus. He stayed there for 4 nights and then flew to Beirut. My brother had a relative in Beirut with whom my nephew spent the next 9 days.

Civil War was raging in Beirut at the time. He went to the American Embassy to try to get a visa. The Embassy official gave him news he didn't want to hear but was the best advice he could have received. The official was frank with him. There was a long process involved in obtaining a visa, and between the Civil War and the "Jewish" issue, my nephew wouldn't be safe sticking around Beirut to wait. The official told him to go to Athens.

My nephew flew to Athens and landed there the Sunday before Memorial Day. He went to the U.S. Embassy on Monday, unaware that it was an American holiday. He returned on Tuesday and started the application process. He reached out to the Athens branch of H.I.A.S. (founded as the Hebrew Immigrant Aid Society), an American nonprofit organization that provides humanitarian aid and assistance to refugees). They helped him find and pay for the room in which he stayed for the next 2 months while waiting for his U.S. visa.

My nephew came to the U.S. on a refugee visa. I sponsored him for a U.S. visa promising that I could support him. He flew to New York and I got him a ticket to continue to Bradley

International Airport in Hartford (Connecticut), our local airport. Estelle met him there on his arrival and brought him to our house.

His mother, maternal grandmother, and younger brother weren't able to get passports so quickly. When they did, they followed my nephew's route from Beirut to Athens and also received help from H.I.A.S. They arrived to this country on Halloween day, 1973. My parents remained in Baghdad hoping for the day that my brother would be freed and they would all be united. This never happened. They eventually left Baghdad in 1976. I bought a house around the corner from us where all of them lived. After a couple of years, all of them, except my parents, relocated to Long Island.

As soon as my nephew came to us, I helped him apply to college. I wanted to do for him what his father could not. I took him to Middlebury and helped with finances, paying any amount not covered by scholarships. I hoped his experience there would be as good as mine. He graduated in 1977. I was delighted that he wanted to become a physician, a surgeon in particular. Once again, I helped him apply to medical schools and assisted with tuition just as I did for my own children. He was accepted New York University School of Medicine. He graduated in 1981 and became a general and vascular surgeon in 1988. During the summers throughout his schooling I brought him to hospitals in the Springfield area, got him internships and introduced him to the medical community.

Today my nephew is in private surgical practice in New Jersey, where he and his wife settled in 1988. They have 3 children and 1 grandchild.

My nephew is a year older than my oldest, Amy. He told Amy what I already knew, that he was so grateful for the love and support I have given him all these years. I am as proud of him as I am of my 5 children. Amy only had inklings of what had happened. I never spoke much about Baghdad to my children until fairly recently. When my older kids were growing up we were in the midst of trauma and upheaval.

My mother continued to be the Rock of Gibraltar, faithfully caring for her husband. At the beginning my father could walk a good distance. They enjoyed walking to the market not far from their home. If Baruch needed to rest, they would rest. When I couldn't drive them to temple, they walked. For years my mother cooked Passover Seders for her family members who could come. Samra lived in town, so she and her husband Bernie brought their 5 boys. Estelle and I brought Nana and our 5 kids. These were large, lively affairs. Since there wasn't much furniture in the house it was easy to string folding tables end upon end to accommodate everyone.

One evening in October of 1978, Baruch and Aliza went to temple for evening services ending the holiday of *Sukkot* (Feast of the Tabernacles marking the end of the harvest). I wasn't available to drive them home and they didn't have a ride, so they walked. It was too much for my father. He had a bad heart attack. I took him by ambulance to the hospital late that night and brought him straight to my very good friend, a cardiologist named Ralph Gianelly (who years later lost his life much too soon). I went back to the hospital early Friday morning and was with my father when he died. He was 84.

We bury quickly and it was Friday. Our entire family flew in from Pennsylvania, New York and Maryland for the early afternoon funeral. All 8 of his children and their families were present.

Early in the book I described how much I enjoyed walking with my father to school in the mornings. We called him "Baba." Each of us have our own memories as is the case in all families, especially large ones.

My sister Samra describes hers:

"He was a real perfectionist, very meticulous. He was haughty. We were afraid of him. He was remote. But his own father was worse! Baba's family was from Mosul, much less progressive than Baghdad. There the man was 'master and controller.' Women had a lesser place. Wives were obedient. We were much closer to my mother's family. They were more fun, broader-minded and gave more credit and opportunity to their wives and daughters.

When I was young, maybe 8 years old, I stole 5 cents from my father's pocket to buy a pickled mango sandwich on the way to school. He knew that 5 cents was missing. He went into a rage. He gave me the spanking of my life. I never forgot it. I swore I'd never take another penny from him. Every Friday, we would go to him and get our weekly allowance. After than episode, I never went to him again. He would have to come and give it to me."

David, the youngest:

"I don't remember my father when he still had his eyesight. All I remember was that he returned from England on an airplane in 1951. He was someone who was well known for business and personal advice and wisdom. My job was to walk him to the café where he met his friends, and bring him home later. My older brothers would take him to the office. He could have left Baghdad in the 1950s with our Uncle Selim's family. I wonder how much his blindness affected his decision to stay as long as he did."

Yeheskel (Baruch's cousin) shared one of his memories with my son. When he was a kid he was playing with someone in the yard. Boys being boys, they made a ruckus. Papa Baruch was trying to take a nap. He snapped at them to keep quiet. Yeheskel learned over the years that Papa Baruch was "*not* to be angered. He was tough."

My mother continued to live in the house by herself. She was always a terrific walker. Much more devout than her husband had been, she walked to temple every day, one arm behind her back. For some reason, she walked on the street instead of the sidewalk. One day in 2003 her neighbor pulled out of his driveway, didn't see her and hit her with his car. She fell and hurt her leg. After that she couldn't be left alone. She needed help during the day and she had trouble sleeping at night. That meant no one with her could get any sleep either. When the helper we hired quit, Samra and I took turns sleeping over, but it became clear that our mother needed to be moved.

We put her in the nursing home very close by. Unfortunately

the only vacancy they had was in the Alzheimer's unit. She would have been much happier living with those who still had their wits about them. She was very unhappy. She kept to herself and took comfort reading her beloved Torah. By and by, she developed chest pain. She was admitted to the Mercy Hospital where she died a few days later at age 94. She was a woman with a will of iron who put her best foot forward through many trials and tribulations.

Hers was a sad ending.

Samra remembers her fondly:

"School was not compulsory in Baghdad, so it was up to my mother to decide when the kids went to school. My father didn't make any of those decisions. She enrolled me late. I don't know why she kept me home longer. Maybe it was because I was her first daughter. In any case, I was at least a year older than all of the kids in my class. She was crazy about education, though. Never having had a chance to go to school, she learned English on her own at the Y.M.C.A. I was really proud of her for doing that. She wrote all of her letters to us in English."

I still think of my mother as fun, energetic and loving. It was very different for my children, who found my parents foreign indeed. I asked them to share their memories:

Amy:

"I was in high school when my grandparents came into our lives. They weren't warm and fuzzy like Nana. I couldn't relate to them. Papa Baruch was blind and didn't speak much English. He was a kindly-looking, stooped old man who always had beads in his hands.

Nana Aliza spoke in broken English with a shrieky voice. Her language improved as time went on, but she still shrieked. There I was, sixteen years old, and all Nana Aliza could say to me was, "Get married! Get married!" I didn't take kindly to that. In her culture I was already an Old Maid.

I admired her for putting on the Passover Seders. It couldn't have been easy for her. We found it strange that she served rice! That's unheard of in the Ashkenazy (Eastern European) tradition. I also admired her strength and perseverance, though at the time, I had no idea what she had gone through. Daddy never talked about Baghdad the whole time I was growing up."

Jonathan:

"I remember riding my 10 speed bike down our hill and around the corner to say goodbye to Papa Baruch before going to camp one summer. Mom suggested/made me go. I knocked on the door. Papa Baruch came to answer it. He still wore his pajamas even though it was afternoon. 'Jonathan,' he said, as he put his hand on me. We sat down for a few minutes in their sitting room next to the kitchen, and I told him that I would be going to summer camp for 2 months. I doubt he had any idea what I was talking about. He had those beads in his hands. I am glad I had the opportunity to see him and speak with him that day, but I certainly agree with Lizzie (my sister) that it was difficult to connect with Nana Aliza and Papa Baruch."

I remember Nana Aliza's religious devotion. She would sing in temple, totally off key but with full-throated vigor and enthusiasm. Fortunately, our family's ability to sing has improved over the generations! (He is referring to the special talent of his sister Elizabeth, opera singer and cantor). Aunt Jeanette remarked last year at her 50th wedding anniversary party that Nana Aliza was the more religious of the two of them. It was she who gathered her strength and kept their family together. Over the years, I was able to communicate better with Nana Aliza. While it was sad to see her become frail, her faith remained strong and sustained her."

Elizabeth:

"I remember how strange they seemed on many levels. He was blind and didn't speak English, so I felt doubly removed. They were from another world, and we didn't know their world. How I wish now we could have known the cultural treasures they were bringing us. We were young, self-centered kids, interested sports and malls!

In their home the chairs were covered with rugs. All the Iraqi women wore gleaming twenty-two karat gold bangles. Nana Aliza had intricate, exquisite jewelry.

For Passover she served date syrup for *haroset,* instead of our usual chopped apple mixed with honey, spices nuts and wine. Both Amy and I remember a lot of okra. We never had it before and we didn't like it. Even the tunes of songs from the *Haggadah,* (the Passover story) used vastly different melodies than our own.

When she was at a service in temple, Nana Aliza would blow kisses to the ark as it was being closed, as if she were saying goodbye to a beloved friend. I don't know if it was a Baghdadi custom or her own. She held great respect and love for the Torah. It was personal. Dad has her same connection to Torah. He enjoys nothing more than sitting down in peace to pray and reflect.

I remember when my grandparents would all call our house. Dad would say *shlonak* (How are you?) and go on and on loudly in Arabic. Although the language sounded both foreign and harsh to me, Dad's voice took on a whole different timbre when he spoke in his native tongue. There is always a smile in Dad's voice when he speaks Arabic. I wish he had taught it to us.

I remember so little of Papa Baruch. I was only 8 years old when he died. Like my siblings I remember his beads. Dad told me that they had nothing to do with prayer. He enjoyed playing with them and rolling them around in his hands, the same way we use worry beads or Chinese balls. They were typical of the culture. Dad said he always used them. It had nothing to do with losing his eyesight."

A group picture of my siblings taken over Elizabeth and David's wedding weekend. Top picture, standing: David, his wife Edna, Maurice, Sami, me, Estelle, Bob Coven (Jeanette's husband) and Bernie Gotlib (Samra's husband). Seated: Samra, Maurice's wife Ann, Sami's wife Monica, and Jeanette. Bottom picture: Bernie (Estelle's brother) with Samra, his wife and my sister.

Part VIII

MY SIBLINGS: AN UPDATE

Here are some postscripts on some of my siblings:

My sister-in-law (my eldest brother's wife):

I neglected to say earlier that my eldest brother (1924-1972) was also sent abroad for college. He attended the University of Beirut for one year. When he came home for the summer, he didn't want to go back. He married over a decade later in June of 1955. As I mentioned previously, he stayed in Baghdad with my parents.

My nephew, his mother and younger brother settled on Long Island. My nephew did his residency in general surgery in a nearby hospital. My sister-in-law never remarried and has lived alone since her youngest child left for college. She continues to work as a secretary.

Samra: (b. 1930, although she has been told it could have been 1929)

Samra met her husband, Estelle's brother Bernie, at our

engagement party. They were married in July of 1959. That same year Samra became a U.S. citizen. Bernie was in the service, stationed in Wiesbaden, Germany. When she finished a project in cancer research, she joined him there. They returned to the U.S. in 1961 and had the first of their 5 sons. After a brief period in Bangor, Maine they settled in the Springfield area. Bernie took over an ear, nose and throat practice from a friend of mine who was retiring. They remained in Springfield until just a few years ago, when they relocated to Florida. They are blessed with 4 grandchildren.

Maurice: (b. 1932)

Maurice came to Boston in 1959 and stayed in the U.S. He earned an advanced degree in mechanical engineering at the University of New Hampshire. Maurice also pursued a Doctor of Science degree at Columbia University in New York. At MIT he did research for NASA. Later, he worked in the Aerospace Division of Westinghouse. Through NASA projects he helped put people on the moon, among other defense programs. He had a high security clearance in the project initially set forth by President Kennedy.

He married his wife, Ann, in 1967. They eventually relocated to Baltimore, settling in Owings Mills for 37 years. Now retired, they live in both Maryland and Florida. They have 2 children and 6 grandchildren.

Rachele: (b. 1935)

Rachele left Baghdad in 1953. She attended Southampton

University in England where she earned a degree in chemistry. She settled on Long Island, New York. She married a man who had been in Maurice's high school class in Baghdad. The marriage ended in divorce. Rachele has 4 children, none of whom are married.

Now in her early 80s, Rachele continues working for the state of New York's social work department in a position that she has held for many years.

Sami: (b. 1938) telling his story to my daughters:

"I am almost 10 years younger than Jake. I remember that after high school Jake went to study shorthand and bookkeeping (that was men's work then). I used to follow him around during the day. I wasn't even in kindergarten yet. Anything Jake did, I did with him. We would paint in the house, we would trim the bushes in the yard together.

There was an incident that has haunted me all my life, something I have never talked about. When I was 9 years old, my older brother drove me to school. All of a sudden there was traffic. We never had traffic. We drove slowly through it. Looking out the window, I saw a Jewish man who had just been hanged. There he was, right in front of me. My brother didn't say a word, as if to erase what we had just seen. As if it never happened at all. Needless to say, I couldn't sleep that night. From then on, my surroundings were like poison.

I was 18 when I left Baghdad in October of 1957. Mentally, I was destroyed. I had to go. My father offered to start up a business for me, but I wanted no part of it. In any case, it was his 'policy' to send his kids abroad for college and I always expected I would go.

At this time it wasn't as bad for the Jews as it had been when Maurice left. They could sell property at market value, but that wasn't as good as it sounds. You were required to put the money in the central (government controlled) bank. They would dole out $200 or $300 a month, just enough to live on. They kept the rest.

It wasn't difficult to obtain a passport. I was of age so I handled the application myself and received the document a month later. I flew KLM to London. Maurice met me at the airport. Three days later I flew on Pan-Am Flight #7 to Boston. Seven is my lucky number!! October 1957, flight #7.

I went to Portsmouth, N.H. to be near Jake. He drove me to the University of New Hampshire and got me admitted. I walked in like a king! When he moved to Boston 2 years later, I transferred to Bentley College where I got my accounting degree in 1964.

My first wife Gail's parents lived outside of Harrisburg, Pennsylvania. Her father helped me get a job as the head of state income tax. It was exactly at that time that the state began charging income tax. I really had a ball doing my job. I stayed in Harrisburg until I retired in 2005.

My second wife, Monica, is British. I met her through friends of my brother David and his wife, Edna. The 3 of them met through mutual friends, Iraqi Jews who settled in Canada. It had been easier for some of the Iraqi Jews to go to Canada since the U.S. quotas were tough.

We now live in Florida. I have 3 children from my first marriage and 4 grandchildren.

Whenever you need advice, you call Jake.
We all love him. His brothers and sisters love him."

David: (b. 1944)

I was 16 when David was born on Yom Kippur in our home. David wasn't yet 3 years old when I left for the U.S. He says, "I only knew (Jake) through photos. I really didn't get to know him until I came to this country."

After one year of college in Baghdad, David left home in June of 1963 at 18 years of age. He had an acceptance to the University of New Hampshire before he had a passport. He remembers that "there were periods of passport issue and periods of closure. It took a full year for me to get my passport – let's really call it an 'exit visa.'"

David flew to Zurich and spent a few days in Lucerne before heading to London to visit relatives. From there he came by sea on the Cunard Line. Maurice spoke to someone in admissions at New York University and helped him get an acceptance. After David spent 3 years there I wrote a letter on his behalf to facilitate his admission to dental school at the University of Buffalo.

David's time in Buffalo coincided with the '67 war in Israel, a very hard time for the Jews still in Iraq. He remembers picking up a newspaper and seeing photos of Jews being hanged in Baghdad.

David settled in New York. Jeanette and Maurice were there and he had Iraqi friends there as well. In 1971 he met and soon married an Iraqi woman named Edna. David set up his periodontics practice in Bloomfield (Connecticut). He splits his time between Connecticut and Florida. He and Edna have 3 children and 6 grandchildren.

Part IX

CONCLUSION

The 1970s came and went. My oldest, Amy, left for college in 1975. Her sister Deborah left home 2 years after that, and Ellen, 3 years later. The younger kids, Jonathan and Elizabeth, attended private schools before college. My financial success allowed me to put all of my children through college and higher education without them having to take any loans. Education was and is of utmost importance to our family and it has been my pleasure to give them that gift.

I am now 90 and fit as a fiddle, though I take an afternoon nap. My mind is sharp and I still play golf. Occasionally I kayak with my kids and grandchildren on Cape Cod, our home for half of the year. In the winter they come visit us in Florida. Estelle and I celebrated our 60th wedding anniversary there on March 18, 2015.

I joyfully toasted my arrival to this country on August 8, 2017, one of the happiest days of my life.

We have had two Cape Cod weddings at the local inn. Elizabeth, an ordained cantor, officiated over the bat mitzvahs

We celebrated my 70th anniversary of my arrival to the United States on August 8, 2017. Amy bought me this hat over the 4th of July and put it away for the occasion.

of two of my grandchildren, Rachel and Sydney, under a tent in our back yard overlooking the ocean. The Falmouth Synagogue, where Elizabeth was cantor for many High Holiday services, lent us a Torah for each occasion. All of my grandchildren have had their bar and bat mitzvah's. The last, Zachary, will have his bar mitzvah in October, 2018.

In this day and age I can be proud to say that all five of my kids married once and continue to be happy with their spouses. I couldn't have hand-picked 5 more wonderful additions to my family. That's not to say we're perfect. Like all large families we ride the waves of autism, cancer, colitis, chronic pain, depression and anxiety. We all have the resilience to cope and continue. We're made of strong stuff.

In my daily prayers I continue to wish only the best for all my family and for peace in this world.

Our 50th wedding anniversary, March 18, 2006

My grandchildren, Thanksgiving, 2015. Left to right: Rachel, Caroline, Amanda, Sarah, Zachary, Ben, Sydney, Naomi, Matthew and Gabbi

Part X

RECENT PHOTOGRAPHS OF MY EXTENDED FAMILY

Amy's family: Caroline, Steven, Amy and Matthew, August, 2012 (Jenny Moloney Photography)

Deborah's family: Ben, Scott, Sydney and Deborah in August, 2012 (Jenny
Moloney Photography)

Ellen's family: The Hotvedts' at home in Minnesota, Thanksgiving Day, 2017: Doug, Rachel, Sarah, Amanda and Ellen

My Middlebury Graduates

Top: Estelle and I with our middle daughter Ellen, 1984. Lower left: My nephew Felix graduated from Middlebury in 1977, though this picture shows his graduation from New York Medical School in 1981. Lower right: Ellen's middle daughter, Amanda, looking great in her cap and gown (2017)

Jonathan's family: Rebecca, Zachary, Gabbi and Jonathan. Naomi forms the top of the pyramid.

Elizabeth and David married on Cape Cod, August 19, 2012. (Jenny Moloney Photography)

Jonathan, Scott, me, Steven and David in August, 2012

Amy, Rebecca, me, Ellen, Elizabeth and Deborah in August, 2012

(Photo by Pat Cohen)

Our Cape Cod Bat Mitzvahs

Rachel (left) and Cantor Elizabeth read prayers during Rachel's Bat Mitzvah on July 9, 2011. The service was held in our back yard on Cape Cod. (photo by Pat Cohen)

Singing at Sydney's Bat Mitzvah on June 29, 2013, again with Cantor Elizabeth on the Cape. From left to right: Elizabeth plays the guitar, Sydney, Rachel, Amanda and Ellen (Photo by Pat Cohen)

The Cantor helps her mother with a passage while I look on. (Photo by Pat Cohen)

Jacob B. Shammash

Passover, March 31, 2018

Part XI

PAINTING A PORTRAIT OF MY FATHER

Now that you have read my father's memoir, I'd like to "paint" my own portrait of him. While we read, we tend to form a picture of a character in our mind's eye given the plot and the author's choice of descriptive words, adding our own imagination to the mix. My portrait is somewhat saucy and irreverent, an informal peek behind the proper façade. As the eldest sibling (I'm now 60) I claim a bit of entitlement.

My dad is a short, thin man with a wiry build, full of kinetic energy with the potential of explosion at any time – usually imminent. Not only is he wiry in physique; the old pictures reveal that he had thick, wiry hair back in the day He lost most of it, as many men do. In the later stages it grew in a peculiar way, resembling one long piece of rope. He expertly wrapped that piece around his head as an Indian would fix his turban. Good LUCK when the wind blew! The nest unraveled and the rope unfurled, flung mercilessly in whichever direction the wind took it. How we laughed.

As for height, he used to say that he was 5'7" inches tall. Looking at him, you might raise your brow and perhaps crinkle a corner of your mouth in an expression of doubt. Duly noting that response, Jake, as he is called, would qualify his calculations, adding "with shoes on."

His skin tone is Mediterranean olive, giving him a healthy, tanned look throughout the most miserable of New England winters. He has been of his time when it comes to an active lifestyle and healthy eating habits. His diet has always been Spartan. When I was young, I'd watch him get ready for work in the morning. He would load up on several pieces of dry toast (who EATS dry toast?!) and grab a few bananas to throw in the car as he headed out for office hours or to one of several hospitals. Oftentimes the dry toast and bananas were all he had during the day unless he found a moment to pick something up at the hospital cafeteria (Once he picked up something much better than food – my mother).

His eating habits weren't so Spartan that he couldn't enjoy the occasional Budweiser beer. I'd climb onto his lap and he'd let me have a sip. I was not impressed. It ranked right up there with getting a kiss before he had a chance to shave. When that happened, I would scamper away, moaning loudly in my retreat while massaging my irritated cheek.

On the rare occasion that we enjoyed my father's presence in the evening, he would read me and my sister Deborah a bedtime story. We had the last laugh, though, because inevitably he fell asleep midsentence and *we* got to stay awake until my mother took over. We especially loved the story he made up for us about a dog named "Little Red Ribbon." We thought it was so special but basically, he took the story of Peter Rabbit and substituted a boy and his dog for the rabbit. The dog escaped from the backyard. To retrieve his beloved pet the boy (like Peter Rabbit) crawled under the fence to fetch him. Doing so, he got hurt. His parents scolded him, forgave him and (like Peter Rabbit) put him to bed *sans* chamomile tea.

My parents had 3 more children after me and Deborah. Ellen was number 3. She was followed by Jonathan. Finally, a BOY! Although I was 8 years old, I still remember the big smile on daddy's face. One would think the family was now complete, but several years later we welcomed Elizabeth. By that time I was in high school and would have preferred a pet cat. Daddy was never big on pets of any kind. He thought animals unclean. I begged for a cat, and his answer was that I didn't need one. I had a new baby sister instead. So my nickname for Elizabeth has always been Cat.

Actually, there *were* some animals that graced out home, albeit very briefly. I begged and begged for a pet. The best I could get was a parakeet, and its cage stayed in the laundry room. We had a couple of them with either blue or green stomachs. Frankly, they were a total bore.

Daddy had and still has a wonderful spirit and sense of humor. On his rare day off, he would take us for a ride. On one of these excursions we landed either on a small farm or an egg store that had chickens. Eight baby chicks just hatched, and they were the cutest things we ever saw. We brought them all home in a box. Mom was not amused. We, on the other hand, were absolutely thrilled. On the eight day they started to fly. That was the end of it. We reluctantly packed them up and took them back from whence they came.

On another excursion we brought our neighbor Jodi with us. Daddy had a plan. "Let's go and buy a baby lamb! We can keep it in the backyard." How lucky could we get! We drove just beyond our town to a more rural area. Daddy stop the car in front of someone's house. He said that one of us should get out and make our inquiry. I was quite timid. Jodi had *chutzpah*, and she was on a mission. Our lamb would be as good as her lamb since there was no boundary between our backyards. Jodi got out and rang the front door of the house. "Hi, do you sell baby lambs?" (Looking back, I can just imagine what the homeowner thought, because clearly, this girl wasn't pulling a prank).

After trying house after house, we were unsuccessful with our attempt to acquire a baby lamb. The day turned out to be a big disappointment for us, but daddy must have been laughing to himself the whole way home.

Each of us are uniquely different, but Elizabeth has a truly special talent. She took up the Suzuki violin method at the age of 3. Her calling became voice. Elizabeth is an opera singer *par excellence*, but teaching aside, it's a tough lifestyle. Daddy coaxed her into a course of study at the Jewish Theological Seminary in New York. She has been an esteemed cantor at a large, conservative temple in Blue Bell, Pennsylvania, near Philadelphia, for over 10 years.

Elizabeth and I, first and last, have a strong connection as the "artsy" members of the family, fine art being my passion. To daddy's delight, 2 of his children, Ellen and Jonathan, chose careers in medicine and each of their spouses are also physicians. Deborah is an accountant. Her husband Scott is our one and only lawyer. Elizabeth's husband David, is a training consultant.

Back to that kinetic energy. Nervous energy. Jacob just can't be still He'll walk around the house looking for something to fix or something to clean. If he gets aggravated we hear the familiar cry, "*Oh, my aching back!*" Anything to avoid neatening the piles of his medical journals or finishing his tax information to get to the accountant (my husband Steven) in time for the April 15th deadline.

Our beloved father has a habit that annoys all of us to this very day. Clearly Jake had an impeccable education from his early years onward. The family, however, is *unclear* as to whether or not he ever learned to tell time back in primary school. Simply put, he has never been on time for anything in his life. We Westerners forget that many cultures "get there when they get there." *Manyana* (tomorrow, meaning later) in Spanish. *Hakuna Matata,* a phrase made famous from the movie "The Lion King," is a Swahili phrase from Central East Africa meaning "no worries." That actually means that *everyone* worries – except Jake.

My husband, Steven, has no idea how my dad ever kept his operating room schedule. In fact, all of us are amazed that he made the boat from Lebanon to emigrate at all. Although the weather made him late for his own wedding, we're positive that even without that issue, he wouldn't have allowed enough time to get there on time. Trying to drag him out of the house for a dinner reservation gives us heartburn before we ever get to the restaurant. Steven (who himself has the terrible habit of glancing at his watch every 5 minutes) growls that my father is still "on Baghdad time."

A perfectionist, everything must be done right, and it won't be right unless Jake does it himself. A good boss knows how to delegate, but daddy prefers to be his own staff. Why waste money calling for help until you're sure you can't fix it yourself? Frugality (in some things) is a virtue.

There are some instances where he puts frugality aside. He is be quick to buy big ticket items, usually when it is something for my mother. One time he went to an estate sale and came back with a huge diamond necklace for his wife. Truth be told, the piece was absolutely hideous. She kindly asked him to return it, and so he did. Years later she'd think about it and say "What was I *thinking*?! I could have taken that thing apart and made some gorgeous pieces!" That incident was an anomaly because my dad actually has great taste in jewelry and loves to have pieces made for her by her favorite jeweler. I'm sure this inclination came from the Mideastern and Indian concept that gold and diamonds are tantamount to hard currency. That said, not all men are generous to a fault.

Family members have given up suggesting that we go out for ice cream. We've heard the "waste of money" line one too many times. The Cape Cod freezers are always stocked with half gallons of a few different kinds (including pistachio, his favorite) bought on sale, as everything should be bought.

I remember an occasion when Deborah invited a bunch of her co-workers to Cape Cod on a Saturday to enjoy our house, poised over the ocean with the most beautiful view a back yard could have. For the evening activity, going out to a movie came under discussion. Daddy caught wind of that. "Why go to a movie and spend all that money! You can rent a movie and watch it right here!" One of the guests leaned over to Deborah and told her she couldn't understand why a man who could afford to live on oceanfront property could get so distressed about buying a few movie tickets.

Jake is neat, clean and fastidious. A retired surgeon, he still scrubs up to the elbows before sitting down to dinner. Helping with the dishes after the meal, however, wasn't even a remote consideration until years after his retirement. One day, my mother woke up and had an epiphany. Now that her husband of 50 years had time on his hands, couldn't he help clean up the kitchen?!

Having fun on Cape Cod

Top: The joggers return for Steven's famous omelets. Left to right: Doug, Steven, Rebecca, Jonathan and Ellen. Bottom: Kayaking with Amy. Still going strong!

Learning new skills in retirement

After dinner that night, she brought him into the kitchen, placed him in front of the sink and told him to wash a pot. He couldn't do it. "Why not?" she asked. "Because I don't know how." On that note, he slunk out of the kitchen to attend to things he *could* do. Estelle thought long and hard about the situation. If he could open up a chest and conduct lengthy operations, *surely* he should be capable of washing a pot. She shared her supposition with her husband, who was forced to admit after hemming and hawing that he really didn't *want* to wash the pot. The reader will hardly be surprised when I say that these days, my father can often be found in front of the sink. From the looks of the picture on the opposite page, he seems to be enjoying it!

For a man who can't sit still all week, come Saturday, the *Shabbat*, he puts everything aside. He sits down with his bible in the living room and tunes out any surrounding ruckus to read, pray and reflect.

There are three wonderful things about my father that I'd like to share. First, he is a charitable human being. From early on he was taught the importance of giving. His desire to help people determined his career path and his destiny. Second, his biggest gift to all who know him is his possession of a very rare quality: compassion.

Third (and I am envious), and he is the most photogenic person on earth. He always takes a great picture.

Amy S. Dane
April, 2018

Book Club Discussion Topics

Amy S. Dane

I would suggest having different members of your book club pick a particular topic of interest to them, share their experiences and conduct a broader discussion.

Writing a memoir:

Having read my father's memoir, what left a lasting impression? What did you gain from reading it? If you could ask him questions, what would you want to know?

Have you ever considered writing your memoir? What would be the advantages of doing so? Who would you be writing it for? How would it resonate for future generations?

All of us have skeletons in our closet. (For example, my father didn't talk to us about what happened to his family in Baghdad. My maternal grandmother's mother was "killed by Russians." She wouldn't talk about what happened). Is it better to keep secrets or to bring skeletons out of the closet and "clear the air?" What would either choice mean for your family and a wider audience?

The family:

Every sibling has a number in the pecking order. My father was the third of nine siblings. Each one had different experiences. How did my father view different family members? How did some of his siblings view the same people? This was a patriarchal society. Were women given the same opportunities as men in the Shamash family?

Immigration:

All of us have immigration stories in our families. We are a nation of immigrants, a "melting pot." This is the tie that binds Americans together.

Discuss my father's journey and compare it to some of his sibling's experiences, particularly that of Maurice. Within only 4 years what made their journeys so different?

Have a member of your book club discuss their immigration story. Explore different scenarios of why people leave their homeland. How do they keep their traditions and practice their religion in a new country?

Immigrants form a diaspora. Some are more successful than others. Why was the Jewish Babylonian diaspora successful? What are some of the different ethnic communities close to your home? How are they perceived in the wider community? What is it like to be an ethnic minority in different parts of the world? Discuss some current immigration "hot spots."

Minorities:

Describe the change in status over time for Jews in Iraq. Address some of the many factors that led to the demise of this population. Minority communities, although initially well established, can become fragile. Talk about some ethnic peoples around the world that are in danger.

Value systems:

What were some of the values held dear in the Shamash household and in the Jewish community in general? How did those values serve them over time? Different ethnicities have different value systems and each individual family has their own. Share some of yours.

Religious rituals:

My father described his daily prayer practice, a typical Passover Seder and some customs surrounding death in Baghdad. Describe some of your favorite religious festivals and rituals. Have some book club members research and share some customs of other cultures.

Acknowledgments

I would like to thank Ellen Peck, a close family friend, for her interest in my story and her help in bringing it to fruition. Ellen currently leads an autobiographical writing course at a continuing education program in Amherst, Massachusetts. She helps people shape and express their stories. Mine was of special interest to her because she felt that many people, herself included, were unaware of the plight of the Iraqi Jews. She didn't know when the Jewish community began in Iraq, nor had she ever heard about the Farhud. She was eager to learn more and hopes that readers of the book will also benefit. She contributed an insightful historical context and time line.

Printed in the United States
By Bookmasters